FANTASIES CAN SET YOU FREE

Fantasies Can Set You Free

Stan Dale
and Val Beauchamp

Celestial Arts
Millbrae, California

Celestial Arts
231 Adrian Road
Millbrae, CA 94030

First Printing, August 1980

Cover design: Betsy Bruneau
Cover photograph: Mike Powers

Manufactured in the United States of America

Library of Congress Cataloging in Publication Data

Dale, Stan, 1929–
    Fantasies can set you free.

    1. Success.   2. Fantasy—Therapeutic use.
3. Fear.   I. Title.
BF637.S8D28   158'.1   80-66195
ISBN 0-89087-268-6 (pbk.)

    2   3   4   5   6   7   86   85   84   83   82   81

Dedicated to:

- Eric Berne, M.D., deceased, whose vision of "The Games People Play" helped me remove my blinders.
- Claude Steiner, whose social consciousness is making this a better world.
- Steve Porter, poet, deceased at 18—and his murderer—the former because if he had understood how awesome was the power of his fantasies he might still be alive, and not just in the memories of those who loved him; and the latter, whose negative fantasies created the act that destroyed the young poet.
- Ida Porter, who at 86 taught me you're never too old to grow.
- Helen Porter Dale, who taught me my humanity, and gentility.
- Janet Crouse, who constantly reminds me that my little "natural child" lives.
- Val Beauchamp, the actualizer of this book, and a grand woman.
- Marsha, Mona, Dan, Rex, Mark, and Scott Dale—outstanding human beings.

and with special thanks to:
Judy Johnstone, word surgeon *par excellence,*
Georgeann Wright, who typed the manuscript,
the staff at Celestial Arts—all of them warm, human, and concerned,
and to the 8,000 men and women who have attended the Stan Dale Sex Workshop and transcended their fears and taught me how, too.

CONTENTS

Those roses under my window make no reference to former roses or to better ones; they are for what they are; they exist with God today. There is no time for them. There is simply the rose; it is perfect in every moment of its existence . . . But man postpones or remembers; he does not live in the present, but with reverted eye laments the past, or, heedless of the riches that surround him, stands on tiptoe to foresee the future. He cannot be happy and strong until he too lives with nature in the present, above time.

SELF-RELIANCE
Ralph Waldo Emerson

PREFACE

For thirty-eight years I was a walking package of fears: fearful that the country was slipping into communism, that it would be taken over by radicals and hippies, that subversive elements were undermining our righteous military goals in Vietnam; and, closer to home, that other men would surpass me professionally, and that my four sons would fail to become the fine, upstanding successes I expected them to be.

Fear had become a habit, as much a part of me as my shadow, and as little noticed. In childhood I was constantly reminded that I was stupid, and one of my fears as an adult was that people would find this out. The only thing I excelled in, I thought, was concealing my stupidity by clever talk and an air of superiority that intimidated potential competitors. At home I played the role of supermacho. Wasn't this the way real men were supposed to act?

Then in 1968 my pat world collapsed around me. In a few short months of devastatingly brutal revelations, all my cherished beliefs proved false. My archconservative political views and all my laboriously gained professional training in orthodox psychology suddenly were revealed as worthless, even harmful.

First to be smashed in one pell-mell week was my political philosophy. It was August in Chicago, and I was assigned by ABC network radio to broadcast street news and commentary on the 1968 Democratic National Convention. The city was tense and no one knew what to expect. The assassinations earlier in the year of Martin Luther King and Robert Kennedy had touched off rioting in cities across the country, and now there were rumors that radical groups were planning violence in the streets to coincide with the convention. Everything in me was braced for trouble from these hordes of dropouts, misfits, and ne'er-do-wells who were invading my city. Reports of their smoking pot, drinking wine, defecating, and even having sexual intercourse in the public parks seemed to confirm my belief that the end of civilization was near.

Grimly I gathered up my protective insignia—press pass, arm band, and tape recorder—and went out into State Street to watch a march of antiwar activists who had come to show their support of Senator Eugene McCarthy and to plead for a peace plank in the party platform. I stared in disapproval at a ragtag procession of bearded and longhaired young people in clothes that could only have come from attic trunks or secondhand clothing shops. Some wheeled baby carriages or held the hand of a child trudging alongside. I was surprised to see an occasional older face—weren't all the troublemakers under thirty?

Abruptly the front line of marchers came to a confused halt, the ones following bunching up behind the leaders. I saw that a cordon of broadbacked policemen was pushing the line back. I ran up to the nearest policeman and asked why the people were being stopped.

"Get your big fat fucking ass out of here!" he yelled.

"Hey, wait, I'm an ABC correspondent . . ."

"Are you going to get your fucking ass out of here before I break it?"

Hardly able to believe my ears, for this was my first encounter with police vilification of *me*, personally, I backed off and went to phone in a report. Afterwards, I hurried on to Michigan Avenue, where I saw a line of National Guardsmen with drawn bayonets. *Bayonets?* My God, I thought, what is this, a civil war? These are just young American kids. Then I noticed an even more stupefying thing. Across the back of each Guardsman was strapped a flamethrower canister. They were planning to control the dissenters by mowing them down with fire! (Only later did I learn that the canisters contained tear gas rather than napalm.)

Days of confusion, uncertainty, and turmoil blurred together. Then one day I arrived at Grant Park to see it become a war zone. Through the crowd I saw a flying wedge of policemen with clubs in attack position burst their way into the now-panicked people, knocking some to the ground, trampling others, the rear of the wedge catching stragglers who had escaped the onslaught of the first attackers.

Suddenly a nearby voice shouted, "They haven't any badges on!" and I looked at the bare lapels of the officers. Had they removed the badges to assure their own anonymity or were they not policemen at all—how could I ever know? The scene I had just witnessed with horror and grief had rocked me off my foundations. As I left the battleground of Grant Park, occasional shots rang out, sirens wailed, soldiers charged about in battle gear with drawn bayonets, and battered civilians were carted on stretchers to first-aid stations or ambulances.

Back at the station I went on the air and reported everything just as I had seen it, sparing nothing. I labeled the affair for what it was—a police riot. For this act I was called on the carpet by the station manager and summarily fired.

My lifelong habit of fear could no longer be taken for

granted. I had seen fear in the street people and in the faces of the police. The police were afraid of the war protestors' *ideas*, and in this they reflected the Establishment's hatred of ideas that threatened its authority. Old views were tumbling and unpredictable, frightening change was in the air. Losing my job gave me my own very personal and practical fear with which to contend, as I had a wife and four sons dependent on me.

Just a few months before the Democratic Convention I had completed graduate training in psychology, but I did not yet feel secure enough to launch into private practice. Instead, I tried to fathom all that had occurred in the light of what traditional psychology had taught me, but it was impossible. Throughout all the writings of Freud, Jung, Adler, *et al.*, fear was treated as a symptom, not a cause.

Now I was beginning to suspect that fear was the basis of all human problems, and I was discouraged and puzzled to find no confirmation of this idea in the literature of my field. Just as I reached an all-time emotional low, I encountered the views of Dr. Eric Berne, who had devised a new psychological concept that he called Transactional Analysis.*

TA proved to be the tool I needed for the reevaluation and transformation of both my personal and professional life. As most people know by now, TA shows that each of us is made up of three psychological entities—the Parent, the Adult, and the Child. The Parent part of us contains everything we have been taught, good or bad; the Adult is the logical, problem-solving part; and the Child is the emotional, feeling part. All human beings function from one or another of these three states of mind. Out of this new understanding, I could now identify in other people and in myself what we were at any given moment: a frightened Child, a critical Parent, or a rational Adult.

---

*Rather than describe TA here, let me recommend *Born to Win*, by Muriel James and Dorothy Jongeward, and *Scripts People Live*, by Claude Steiner.

At this point I began to recognize fear for what it is: the most destructive power on earth. My attitudes and beliefs were forced to make a complete turnaround, and I actually became a different person. Thus commenced the perplexing, unguided, fascinating, and endless trip that will keep unfolding itself before me every single moment until the day I die.

What 1968 did for me was to confront me with every aspect of my life and make me look at my Parent, Adult, and Child. The result has been a sense of clarity and of potency that makes each day a joy to live. It's true, as my son says, that Utopia lies just between our ears.

Stan Dale
Santa Rosa, California
Autumn, 1980

INTRODUCTION

Since the beginning, humans have had fantasies. They are called by various names: visions, dreams, thoughts, imaginations, theories, hypotheses and the like.

And since the begnning, people have been attempting to explain the thinking process with a variety of fantasies: inspired, demonic, possessed, evil, subconscious, ego, id, superego, ad infinitum.

The dictionary and the Bible are both works of fantasy, yet they dictate a "reality" every day to millions of people. In other cultures similar books do likewise.

Every book ever written, every motion picture, radio and TV program is but a fantasy created "between the ears" and the effect on humanity has been astounding.

Today we may still be like the proverbial three blind men attempting to describe an elephant by feeling only its left hind leg or its trunk or its tail when it comes to the human mind. But one thing is known at this time: the major function of the human mind is to fantasize—create mental images and, to most of us, we take that mental image as a reality and "run with it," as if it were indeed a reality. To the possessor of the fantasy *it is* a reality.

To Freud, the ego, id, and superego were realities, and millions of people in many countries started using the terms as if there really were an ego to be bruised, an id loaded with both latent and boiling sexuality, and a super-ego that overrode everything.

The word "subconscious" is likely to connote deep rivers, streams and sewers loaded with all manner of mental garbage.

In recent times we have created snake pits to throw human beings into and have called them hospitals, rather than admit that these people held up powerful mirrors to us. We didn't know what was wrong with them, but we sure didn't want to be like them. So, instead of admitting we didn't know how to treat them, we locked them up and threw away the key.

The same goes for criminals. We have, for much too long now, been treating the symptoms rather than the cause. Once again, these people hold up powerful mirrors and we don't want to look, lest we realize that every heinous act, every "crazy behavior" ever performed, we, too, are capable of committing.

No one is immune!

These "vile" creatures," these "crazy weirdos"— were they not little babies once? At least most of them are now called *sick.* That's an improvement over the past. Or is it?

Ten million alcoholics, millions of other problem drinkers and drug users, and we still call them *sick.* We look to doctors, benevolent fathers and mothers, gods in their own right, to cure them and make them well again.

They administer drugs, shock treatment and cut out portions of brains and call themselves advanced and progressive. Do you see the awesome power of fantasy?

What we don't understand, we attempt to fit into preformed, prelabelled boxes and if it doesn't fit, we may have to chop off an arm, leg or part of a head to make it fit, but fit it will!

Every person on this planet has had problems and "crazy" spells at some time in their lives, but very few of

us have had the tools—the understanding and awareness—that it takes to overcome the ones that overcome us.

We either coast, "go crazy," have a nervous break-
down (don't you love the mental image a nervous break-
down elicits—millions of little nerves breaking down like a
machine's parts falling out?) or take ourselves to a doctor,
"a shrink" or a counsellor.

Many of them, with their professional organizations,
will even use the police to protect their exalted positions
and woe to anyone who may question these gods as to their
procedures and nostrums.

There have been the few throughout the ages who
have made it to "the mountain top" and sounded the
alarm. Some heeded; some labeled them crazy or heretic.

One of these, Eric Berne, said, in effect, thanks Freud,
you were a revolutionary and a trailblazer for your time,
but now it is time to travel yet another path.

That there is a definite cause-effect relationship for all
human behavior, and the cause, microscopic and blurred
as it may be at times, still eludes us, (because it may be a
fleeting fantasy, made in the earliest days of childhood or,
maybe, a recent one that we're not in the least bit aware
of) but it is there nevertheless.

The purpose of this book is not to put down or belittle
those who have gone before. They did only what they knew
to do. Some manipulated, schemed and did great harm to
human beings in the name of society or psychiatry, but,
there too, I am more interested in the cause, not the effect.
Pat answers that used to be there to guide us have with-
ered and crumbled and joined the sands of time. Gods that
we once created, we now question. Likewise, values. So
where are we and where are we going?

The joyousness of fantasy is that there are no boundaries really, except those we impose on ourselves. Take national boundaries, for example—pure fantasy at work, for
where on a spinning planet do you arbitrarily draw lines?
Where on a spinning planet is up or down? Where is there

really time, if not only in the human mind? And so, with the new awareness and understanding that everything we see and perceive and think takes place right between your ears, and that those ears belong to you and only you, take this opportunity to rebuild and restructure yourself and your planet, and, yes, even the rest of the universe, with only one injunction: *Never violate the sovereignty of others.* Know that no one is crazy or a born criminal. We only *act* that way and one day we'll get at the cause, not the effect.

Know that it is never too late to change, that the human mind can create anything it sets its mind to, and all that has been negative in the past can be positive from this second on.

That is the awesome power of fantasy.

1

THE AWESOME POWER
OF FANTASY

That fear is the most destructive of all emotions has been proved over and over for years in both my personal and professional life. Everybody has fears. I'm sure that you, too, have fears from which you would like to free yourself. You made a decision long ago to give these fears a good home, and then they assumed command and have been your master ever since. Well, you invited them in, and you are the only one who can give them their walking papers. You need to know only one thing in order to do this.

FEAR IS A FANTASY.

Fear, that supreme crippler of the human spirit, is a creation of the imagination. Because our minds are boundlessly creative, we can conquer fear by converting an unwanted fantasy into a desirable one.

The untapped power residing in human fantasy is comparable to the untapped energy in the ocean's tides. Understanding and using the power of fantasy can reshape your outlook, personality, disposition, and ultimately your life. You can rid yourself of emotional handicaps acquired in the past and release the real person who has been afraid to come out. These are not idle theories, they are actualities experienced by people who were adventurous enough to try to transform their lives. In my own life the power of fantasies has effected a total transformation for which I will be forever grateful.

I was well aware of the destructive power of fear by the time I had fully dealt with the questions raised in my life by the Chicago experience. That fear originates in fantasy, however, did not occur to me until two years later, and then only by chance.

A large adult audience was listening to my talk on Eric Berne's book, *Sex in Human Loving*. As usual, I was using explicit language. (After all, there is little point in trying to inform people if you must avoid the vocabulary that precisely describes the situation!) But I began to notice some curious reactions. A few were listening quietly, but some people were frowning and restless, and still others hunched their shoulders and arms close to their bodies as if fearing an attack. Why this hostility? Then I realized why: I had used the word *fuck*.

"If you're hung up on the word *fuck*," I said impulsively, "chances are you're fucking up your fucking!"

A gasp ran through the entire room. Then a woman stood up and shouted, "If there's a decent man here, he'll punch you in the mouth for using language like that in front of us ladies!" Other women and a few men rallied to her support, but some voices shouted, "Aw, shut up and sit down! Let's hear him talk!"

I stared, not believing what I had stirred up. People were screaming and waving their fists, their eyes wild. I was looking at *fear*! These people were acting like maniacs because they were afraid of a word. It was a simple word, known by everyone and used for centuries—a word that couldn't possibly harm anyone—yet these people were behaving as if I'd turned a rattlesnake loose among them.

Fear was destroying their common sense, and yet that fear came out of their own lively and creative imagination. In a stunning realization, I knew then that *fear* was the dirty four-letter word, and that fear was born in a *fantasy of the mind.*

That incident stayed in my mind and I thought long and deeply about its implications. I came to see that fear is the emotion that destroys human beings by making them timid, unsure, and self-deprecating; by holding them back from realizing their fullest potential; by creating hatred and suspicion; and, worst of all, by depriving them of a joy few people ever experience—open, honest communication and true intimacy with others.

But how can we control fear? From time immemorial, this destructive emotion has been around to plague us. Must we tolerate it forever?

The conviction that fear is a fantasy kept recurring. If fear originates in a fantasy, might it not be overcome with another fantasy? If one emotion is a creation of the human mind, all emotions and all thoughts are also mental creations. At last I was on the right track. Here was the tool for overcoming fear: *The mind invents fear, a destructive fantasy, and the mind can equally well invent a constructive fantasy.*

The fear fantasy is triggered by a recollection of danger, or by an outside stimulus that suggests the idea of a danger, or presents an actual danger. The mind then instantly creates its own emotional reaction of fear. The danger, whether present or merely expected, is not the creator of the fear. The fear originates in and is created by the mind of the person perceiving the danger.

This process of the mind applies equally to all emotions, such as anger, sadness, or jealousy. Feeling anger does not mean you have to be violent. Feeling sadness does not mean you have to be so depressed you jump from a high building. Feeling jealousy does not mean you have to claw the eyes out of your rival, or your lover. It is natural and healthy to experience an emotion, but what you do next determines whether you succumb to the emotion or master it. Feel your feelings, but think before you act. Helping you over this hurdle will be one of the major concerns of this book.

The human mind is the most creative instrument we know. Every single thing built, invented, or thought down through the ages has been a product of imagination, a fantasy in someone's mind. The earliest human beings' pots and tools, the Greek temples, and today's computers—all the result of fantasies. All religions, philosophies, government systems, sciences, inventions, architecture, art, music—everything that men and women have dreamed of and brought to fruition is a product of fantasy.

Fantasy is the mind at play, the highest form of mental activity. Nowhere in this book will the word *fantasy* mean something unreal or of no value. Fantasy is as real as life itself and as valuable; without fantasy life would not be worth living. Deprived of it we would be that dread thing, a human vegetable.

Fantasy is the very essence of humanity, the source of all joy, love, self-confidence, faith, creativity, and aspiration. But fantasy also produces the dark side of that coin: unhappiness, hate, self-doubt, anger, fear, and despair. Destructive emotions and acts require as much creative imagination as constructive ones.

How can the same mental process breed such opposite results? It is because fantasies themselves can be positive or negative. Simply stated, your positive fantasy is one that makes you feel good, and your negative fantasy is one that makes you feel bad. The desirability of creating positive fantasies is obvious. That anyone would choose to fantasize negatively seems illogical, even unbelievable, yet most people do so choose.

Because fear is the product of fantasy, and because your fantasy of fear originates in your brain, you have sole and complete authority over it. You can hang on to the fear, or you can dismiss it and substitute another fantasy.

What you do with your fantasy of fear, or with any feeling, determines what you are at that moment in your life. You can be a cringing, fearful victim of your own fantasy, or you can be in charge of the situation confronting you. Whichever you choose, your fantasy is powerful. Fantasies can destroy as easily as they serve.

Choice is the key factor. By deciding to choose one way rather than another, you can replace what you don't need or want for what you do. Choose well. You have a powerful tool at your command. I call it the awesome power of fantasy.

2

THE REAL POWER TRIP

At the heart of human happiness is personal power, the OKness inherent in every human being. Traditional psychology has bombarded us with endless words about how to achieve happiness, but nowhere in all this clutter have I found any awareness of what I am convinced is the essence of human dignity and self-esteem: personal power, or potency.

Orthodox methods deal with symptoms, trying to patch up once-potent psyches. The surface indications that are *results*, rather than *causes*, of problems receive the therapists' attention; hang-ups, fixations, obsessions, compulsions, and other gobbledygook get the spotlight. The loss of power (or even its existence) in the troubled individual is overlooked.

Though I have used the word *power*, actually I prefer the word *potency*. Hitler had power, yet he did not have personal potency. He was driven by enormous fear and self-hatred that only total domination of masses of helpless people could assuage. Yet Hitler was born a baby, even as you and I, with a full complement of personal potency that, to the world's everlasting sorrow, he totally surrendered.

By potency, therefore, I do not mean ruthless, devious, or even subtle power over others. Such power diminishes those who exercise it. The bully, the swindler, the gossip all suffer from their demeaning, destructive traits, though they may achieve the upper hand momentarily in human encounters. The potent individual is none of these.

The truly potent person is one who is acutely aware of his or her own power and who does not succumb to fear. Potency is intrinsic and natural, as it grows out of total self-acceptance. The potent person can look in the mirror and rejoice in the face that is uniquely his or her own, not concerned with its meeting some external standard of beauty. (A sightless person can enjoy his or her facial contours through the sense of touch.) The potent individual enjoys and accepts the body that is the vehicle for life and pleasure in this physical world. This person knows she or he is not merely an intellectual being from the neck up, but an extremely alive, physical creature capable of infinite sensations. A potent person with physical disability rejoices that the body is keeping the self, the creative mind, alive.

Potency stimulates all the senses, and potent people go through life intensely aware of their physical surroundings. Rooms and doorways, porches and gardens, streets and bridges, fields and rivers, forests and mountains all have an emotional impact on people who consciously notice them.

Most important, potent people respond to others with love. My definition of love is dignity, respect, trust and understanding of a loved one's needs, wants, and desires. On that assumption, potent people come from a place of love in dealing with all human beings. They may not like certain individuals, or, more accurately, certain aspects of their natures, but they always retain a positive feeling for the inner core, the inherent OKness of that individual.

Think of that inner core as the sun—warmth-giving, life-giving, constant and dependable. We can't always see it, so we say "The sun's not shining today." Yet the sun is *always* shining, even at night. During the day clouds may obscure it, but it still shines.

From babyhood, we piled layers and layers of garbage on the OK core that is our sun. Every time we gave up a natural desire in order to conform (survive), or imitated someone's destructive behavior, we added another layer. Now those layers obscure our OKness, just as clouds obscure the sun. Most people see only the garbage and are not aware of the hidden OKness in everyone, including themselves. This is why so much misunderstanding and conflict exists between individuals. But potent people are not fooled by garbage; they are always in touch with their own core and those of others.

Communication is kept open and clear. In conversation of a personal nature, potent people make frequent use of "I" messages. They say "I feel angry when you do that," rather than "*You* make me so angry!" No one makes another angry; the recipient chooses to be angry—or can choose not to be. Ascribing the anger source to the other only dumps one's own garbage on that person, and increases the conflict.

Potent people always take responsibility for their own feelings. At every moment in life, they choose how to react to the stimulus coming from another person. The potent man can think "Just because he is bad-tempered, I don't have to be." "If she is paying attention to someone else, I don't have to be jealous." The potent woman can think "If he demeans me, I don't have to feel it's a personal insult, but rather understand where he is coming from."

Nor are potent people afraid of being alone. Seldom, if ever, will they be lonely, because they are aware of their own OKness. (There is a great difference between being lonely and being alone. To be in the wretched state of loneliness is a personal choice and it arises out of powerlessness. The lonely person believes he has no options—no friends, no place to go—and he therefore feels powerless to change his situation. So he chooses to be lonely and miserable.) The potent person, when alone, is enjoying the company of someone deeply respected and cared for, an interesting person whose thoughts are entertaining and provocative, and he or she needs nothing or no one to fill the *chosen* solitude. Reading, entertainment, strokes, approval, and the stimulation of another's ideas and personality are always delightful. But they are not necessary. It is a false notion to believe we are wastrels if not constantly doing something, or social failures if not surrounded by friends.

The simple formula for what I have been describing is this: *Awareness plus Experience equals Potency.* Awareness comes about when we allow ourselves to respond fully to everything in our lives. We become acutely conscious of our physical senses, and appreciative of the delightful messages they convey. In addition, we pay close attention to our feelings and emotions. When we have this heightened sensitivity we put it into practice over and over until it is second nature, and it becomes experience. When we reach the point of having combined awareness and experience, we then have the personal power and command over self that I call potency.

Whenever I think of the ultimate in potency, I remember the peaceful face of a Buddhist monk I once knew. He possessed an aura of utter calm and contentment. Was it an aura of actual physical energy as shown in Kirlian photography, or was it a spiritual ambiance so compelling that all who came near could feel its spell? I am not enough of a student of Eastern philosophy to know, but I can never forget the quiet power of this remarkable human being. If ever an individual was potent and supremely OK, this man was the personification of that state of being. He had cast off all the comforts and almost all the necessities of life. He was content to wander alone with only the clothes on his back and an empty cup, fulfilled by the contemplative life, desiring nothing. It is not surprising that many young people here and abroad, disillusioned with the materialism of Western civilization, have turned to the Eastern philosophers. I know that such a way of life would not appeal to most of us. I only mention it as an example of how far the human mind can transcend the ordinary, reaching a state of pure awareness that is almost beyond our comprehension.

Potency can be maintained, however, without renouncing your world. A worthwhile life can be lived even in the midst of much that is antagonistic. Selectivity is the key: deciding which accustomed ways are important to retain, and which are better dropped. The true exercise of potency is making choices. Society will always pressure you to conform; that is the nature of society. Potency is the ability to resist, to think for yourself, and to live accordingly.

At the other extreme from potency are *powerlessness* and its twin followers, *fear* and *anger*. Any situation that goes against us, or any person who seems to control us, may set off a feeling of powerlessness. We seldom recognize this feeling, however, because it is so swiftly followed by fear and anger; these are what we notice. We fantasize what may happen to us as a consequence, and we feel endangered. We are frustrated and furious at our inability to resist.

A woman may worry that her husband will get drunk at a dinner party and disgrace them both. (Worry is a form of fear.) Later, at the party, she may feel anger at his behavior. In both situations, she is positive her feelings are caused by his actions, anticipated or present, whereas their real cause is her feeling of powerlessness. If she had the power to alter his behavior, she would not feel the fear or the anger.

Or the fear may be even greater, as with a person expecting to lose his or her job, but feeling powerless to change the employer's mind.

You might assume it is immaterial which feelings are responsible, since the result is the same. But that assumption would be incorrect. Fear and anger are emotions that block off the rational part of the mind. Rational thinking is impossible, and no sensible course of action may be devised and undertaken. But if powerlessness is seen as the real problem, you can then start to figure how to take back your power (your potency), which somewhere along the way you have relinquished.

Powerlessness is also what compels radical groups to bomb corporate offices and plants. The bombers' intentions are not to kill (they usually warn beforehand), but to bring about a political change they believe desirable. Others may not agree it is desirable, but it is the dissenters' feelings, not their opponents', that originate the action. The radicals feel powerless to effect change by legal routes, so they resort to bombs in order to feel powerful.

Entire countries can feel the powerlessness that produces fear and anger and leads to war. Current prime examples are the unresolved political situations in Northern Ireland and in the Middle East.

On a personal note, I believe it useful here to mention briefly my own struggle to regain potency. Rigid and fearful attitudes and habits of half a lifetime had to be completely wiped out, and clear-thinking, nondestructive ways evolved and put into daily use. All the concepts, conclusions, and recommendations in this book are ones I personally have used and still use, because they work.

Because I have practiced what I preach, I can now honestly say that I am a potent individual, capable of dealing without rancor with virtually any person or situation. I have learned to be direct, and not to make phony excuses for refusing to do something I don't want to do, in the mistaken belief that this will protect someone's feelings. People trained in the socially correct ritual of back-and-forth, "No, thank you," . . . "Oh, but you must!" "No, thanks very much," . . . "My dear, I insist!" and then final capitulation by the reluctant victim, sometimes are taken aback. But if they are true friends, they come around to appreciating a direct answer and may adopt this way themselves. This may seem a trivial matter, but so much of daily life consists of confronting and evaluating the suggestions of other people as to how you or I should spend our time that I believe knowing how and where to draw the line is extremely important. Your life and mine are ours alone to experience, and I quietly and civilly insist on being in charge of mine.

Although I eschew rules as much as possible, one firm rule faithfully observed is: *Never violate another's sovereignty.* Just as I respect my own right to determine what I do (my sovereignty), I respect the same rights in others. My preferences may not always jibe with the preferences of family or friends, but we do our utmost to prevent their clashing by making sure we all have a chance to air our views openly and honestly. It is amazing how insignificant the original conflict usually becomes; most human problems are hard to untangle mainly because neither side understands the other's desires.

I also know for a certainty that no one could influence me to act contrary to my values. Although as a boy I begged to go to military school, then later served in Korea, today it would be impossible for me to kill even if ordered at gunpoint. Unable to prevent my own death, I would not feel powerless, because I would be acutely aware of my power to refuse to kill. I don't want to die any more then the next person, but I don't fear death, just as I have learned not to succumb to fear from any source.

All of this is only to show that it's possible for anyone

to turn his life around. If I had been told twelve years ago how I would change, I honestly wouldn't have believed it. But I'm not trying to change *your* life—that would be oppression on my part, something I am firmly against. I only want to offer options that may not have occurred to you, for the more options we have, the freer we are. Call this book a road map for anyone who cares to travel a similiar road. Positive fantasies can be created by any of us, but they need room in the mind. Negative, destructive fantasies are hoggish; they'll crowd out positive constructive ones every chance they get. But they can also be wiped out in an instant by a positive fantasy—*if you so desire!*

The life most worth living is the life with the most positive fantasies. For that life is truly potent. Who would not desire it?

3

PUTTING YOU
IN THE DRIVER'S SEAT

One of the greatest obstacles to understanding and solving
a personal problem is that the problem never exists only in
the present. If it were a neat package pertaining only to
the here and now, finding a solution might be easy. But
present problems always have ties with the half-remembered past that can interfere with a rational solution.

Dave is aware that something is wrong in his marriage.
His wife's behavior has become erratic, sometimes openly
belligerent, at other times distant and cold. He is afraid to
ask her why, for he dreads the answer. It might confirm
the overwhelming sense of inadequacy that floods him
now. A stream of forgotten incidents from his childhood
rushes through his mind: his father telling him how bad he
was; his teachers ridiculing him; big boys laughing and
shoving him about. No single recollection is clear, but all
together add up to: "You're no good, Dave . . . at last your
wife is seeing you for what you are." He is sure their marital difficulty is his fault, and he has never felt so lacking in
confidence or more afraid. He cannot deal rationally with
the present, because all those old feelings of being inferior
to other people are too strong.

In our society, most people's feeling of self-worth, like
beauty, is only skin-deep. Underneath, clamoring to

emerge at the slightest opportunity, is a great mass of self-doubt and fear. Why? Where does it come from?

Fear is like a mental cancer, often invading the mind so early that it pre-dates conscious memory. But the human brain is an intricate and efficient memory bank that stores every sensation received from the moment of birth. It has a memory-storage capacity of roughly 14 billion synapses (separate, microscopic "cubbyholes" for each impulse). Repetition of the same sensation physically deepens and strengthens the neuronal pathways of the brain. This is how habits are developed—automatic ones like driving a car, typewriting, playing a musical instrument, and less automatic but familiar ones of daily living, like going to the same job each morning and returning to the same home at night.

No imprint of any experience is ever lost; most are not consciously remembered, but all are capable of being aroused, given the proper stimulus. We continually call thousands into awareness as we go about the business of everyday activity, but thousands more are activated in ways less appropriate.

These are the stored experience of infancy and child-hood—some pleasant, like suckling the breast of the mother, hearing her coos and seeing her approving smiles, and being soothingly rocked in her arms. But some are fearful—loud, angry voices, slaps and spanks, or insults and ridicule. The unconscious mind still remembers these hurts and the fear they once caused, even though the individual may not be consciously aware of them now.

But something in adult life that bears a slight resemblance to negative experiences of the past can suddenly revive the feelings of fear that accompanied them. The person feels a tidal wave of emotion all out of proportion to the present situation, for the adrenal glands immediately react by releasing a surge of adrenaline throughout the body. *The body responds equally to real or imagined danger.* Just thinking of something that particularly frightens you may cause you to feel pressure in your throat and chest, and the sweat glands in your palms to activate.

Therefore, when a wave of fear whose source is in the long-ago surges through your mind and body, your first impulse is to respond emotionally. Those old fears are saying you are not smart enough or lovable enough to deserve better treatment.

Out of my own experience, I know it is possible to deal with and overcome such fears.

The next time you are in the clutches of a fear that makes no sense or is only a vague, nervous feeling that keeps you from doing what you really want to do, stop and look squarely at it. Then follow these steps:

1. Allow yourself to experience the fear fully.

2. Ask yourself some essential questions about it.

3. Take complete responsibility for resolving it by yourself.

Never sit on your emotions! Don't suppress fear. Feel your fear keenly, fully, and deeply, until you can scarcely bear the feeling. Experience every part of the fear and pain: all the old embarrassment, humiliation, confusion, hurt, and betrayal. Experience, too, the terror you once felt as a child, which has just now resurfaced to set off a new panic in your head and gut.

If those feelings mount until you want to scream, go ahead and scream. Or, breathe deeply five or six times, punch a pillow, run around the block—anything to burn off the excess adrenaline. Inform others who may be present that you are not angry at them, having a tantrum, or going crazy—you are only letting off steam. There is nothing to be ashamed of in all this. Your fears have been building up in your head ever since infancy; they're dug in (part of you likes having them there!) and they won't disappear with a polite wave of the hand. It will take guts and perseverance to get rid of them, but it's supremely worth it.

An invaluable aid at this point is to use the reporter's checklist of essentials: Who? What? When? Where? Why? and How? Go off by yourself and ask the following questions: Who am I? What am I doing? What am I afraid of? How did this mental state get started? How did I begin fantasizing this way? What am I getting out of this? What perverse payoff am I secretly enjoying from my fear? Don't ask too many "why" questions; they tend to turn into self-harassment (like, why are you so stupid?) Finally, ask youself, *when do I intend to stop?*

Ask yourself the questions out lout and answer them out loud. Spoken words clarify jumbled feelings. Our up-bringing ridicules solitary speech and in the early days of my self-discovery and re-education I would catch myself talking alone, then guiltily look over my shoulder at imaginary eavesdroppers, wondering if I were going crazy. After a while, however, I saw that verbalizing feelings and thoughts provided a breakthrough to understanding them. It is a habit I still follow and which I recommend to you.

Sometimes there is a tiny grain of truth in a negative fantasy, a fear that has a plausible foundation. If so, this is reality, and we can always deal with reality. Deal with that grain of truth in your negative fantasy as forthrightly and energetically as you would tackle the fallen timbers and furnishings of your house after an earthquake. The reality in your fear cannot be dismissed, and it will continue to hold you back unless you deal with it. Its cause may lie within your own nature, or it may come from your justified suspicion of another person's feeling or behavior. If it is from the latter, honest communication is the answer.

People may be trying to fill you with their negative fears. *Never accept another person's negative fantasy!*

This is one of the few cardinal rules for maintaining your own potency.

There may be times when fear seems just too overpowering to handle rationally. You may be physically tired (fatigue is often the result of emotional stress). Just change channels as if your mind were a television set; find a better program by deliberately switching to a new positive fantasy or change channels by saying "To hell with it!" and take a walk.

You may be tempted at times of lowered energy to rebuke yourself with, "Don't be silly! You shouldn't be afraid!" Resist that temptation like the plague! *Shoulds* and *shouldn'ts* are Parent words. Watch out for them.

If you ask "What am I getting out of being afraid?" your honest answer will probably be "I'm making people take care of me. I'm getting attention, strokes, plus affirmation of my fears. That's what I want most—to hear that my fears are justified and that life handed me a raw deal. Poor little me!"

Now, everyone's first reaction to your depression or fear is to put a loving arm around you and say, "Don't be afraid! It's all right, you'll get over it." But that kind of comfort is actually only another payoff. It doesn't deal with the cause, so it doesn't change anything.

You cannot work your way through to self-understanding unless you are willing to take full responsibility for it. Other people's comfort is appropriate when we are in a real crisis and suffering pain or anguish. These situations are very different from ones where suffering is caused by negative fantasies. Then dependency on others for sympathy only provides an excuse for avoiding emotional work that only you can do. Millions of people do not possess potency. They do not really live, they merely survive, passive travelers on the journey from birth to death; out of fear, they let others tell them where and how to go. But it is never too late to move up into the driver's seat of your own life-vehicle.

To stop being a victim, you must demystify your mind and set it free. You can fool the world, but if you pretend that you are happy in that refuge your are cheating yourself. You'll never find out your real potential, or the depth and variety of feelings of which you are capable. You'll never know what exciting and illuminating experiences you might have had. Being straight with yourself is the prime requirement.

The steps I have outlined for identifying an unwelcome fear will become a natural response after sufficient practice. Repeating an action establishes a habit, for our brains are built to make the action easier with each repetition. The secret is to follow this procedure *every time* an illogical fear arises. It is one thing to decide to change one's attitude while pondering quietly and alone, and quite another to respond instantly and rationally in the thick of the fray. Once having established the new habit, however, you will experience an unmatched sense of well-being.

4

BORN FEARLESS

Every man and woman on this planet was born fearless. Each one of us was a ball of energy, gloriously potent and completely lacking in fear. Look at a baby. It is totally un-self-conscious. It may stare at you or turn its head away. It yawns or burps or urinates or defecates whenever the urge arises. It is untrained in polite behavior and does exactly as it pleases. But by the time a baby becomes an adult, it will have been taught a thousand fears. The deplorable result is that the continuous impact of fear will have eroded much of the inherent potency of the child and destroyed the potential to become the joyous, fulfilled person nature intended.

Human failures are everywhere; some people are able to conceal their failure, others cannot. The wino staggering into a flophouse, the shopping-bag lady going from trash bin to garbage can, the well-tailored bank president attaching a hose to the car's exhaust—all three came into this world possessing the vibrant potency of the newborn, and all were born without the knowledge of fear.

Now each is afraid, alone, alienated from human contact. Someone educated them to feel fear, and they learned their lessons well. They gave their original power away in increments, and now self-esteem has vanished and they are powerless. All that is left is fear.

Though not always so tragically, we are all victims of a loss of potency because we have been trained to fear. Have you visited a high school classroom lately? As you observed that roomful of youthful faces, did you wonder at the real thoughts and feelings behind each face? Get close enough to gain the trust of an adolescent and you will find that scarcely one girl or boy is free of daily fears.

Young people cover their fears well as a rule, with bravado or insolence or super-politeness, or by retreating into aloofness. But behind these brave fronts they struggle with the fears of low grades and social failure, not to mention their teachers, the principal, the coach, or one or both parents.

Above all, they fear each other. Craving to be popular, they torment themselves with worry over their unpredictable complexions, the shapes of their noses or their bodies, their inability to be witty in a group, or their embarrassment at being too clever and committing a gaffe. But their burgeoning sexuality is the source of greatest anxiety and fear. Warned to postpone all interest in their own sexual feelings and those of the other sex (heaven forbid, of the same sex), yet bombarded by seductive television and magazine advertisements, they are constantly confused. Today's teenage boys and girls are in the bind of being damned if they do and damned if they don't, and their moods alternate between guilty fear and daring daydreams.

What of their parents, who have supposedly put behind them all youthful uncertainties? Added years do not automatically bring greater understanding. Most men and women are handicapped by sexual ignorance, misinformation, and fears carried over from childhood. Nor is sexual disappointment the only source of anxiety among adults.

Always considered the braver sex, men, in fact, labor under never-ending fears, great and trivial, but they have been trained to conceal fear. This may be bravery, but it exacts its toll. The fear is suppressed only from public view; inside it churns around, preventing the man from giving his calm, undivided attention to the very task about which he worries. Prestige and money are the chief concerns of many men, and in the commercial world where these rewards are most likely to be found, ulcers, migraine headaches, high blood pressure, strokes, and heart attacks claim as many victims as fortune favors. Even the fear of such calamities makes them more probable. Working women have such fears, too, but to a lesser degree, for women have not been trained from childhood, as men have, that their identity lies in their vocation. Employed or not, most women's identity is as wife, mother, and her fears center on the welfare of her children. Yet to any who believe these fears are proof of being conscientious, I want to say: All fear is destructive, and there are better ways to prevent trouble than to fear it.

Women used to be less susceptible to the pressures of the business world, but an unfortunate side effect of the movement to liberate women has been their increasing vulnerability to the ailments formerly afflicting men only. The care of children and the home has traditionally been the province of women, and there are many uncertainties inherent in that vocation. In this period of transition to a more balanced sharing of life's work between men and women, however, many women now find themselves "liberated" to work for income while still carrying the responsibilities of their traditional role in the home.

Fear is no less a tyrant over older men and women, and may even grow more oppressive. The attitudes and habits ingrained in youth do not disappear with age, but tend to become more firmly fixed, and are often carried to the grave. It is true that increased years bring on anxieties seldom considered before: retirement, ill health, diminished muscular vigor, lessened ambition and drive, aging appearance, decreased sexual opportunities, and, most of all, loneliness and the fear of death. All these new fears, added to those from younger days, do indeed seem formidable.

In fact, fear is probably the emotion most frequently felt by every person, young or old! Hearing the morning alarm, who does not feel a slight fear at the unknown events of the coming day and wish to snatch a few more minutes of blissful unawareness? Then there is the hurried dressing and breakfast, for fear of not getting to work on time. You fear the children are malnourished because they skimp on breakfast, then send them off to school with anxious warnings to be careful crossing streets. They scarcely hear you, but without this daily incantation to ward off calamity, you feel you'd be neglecting your duty.

A hundred unnoticed (but felt) fears occur each day: fear that the traffic light will turn red before you reach the intersection; fear that a mislaid object is lost or stolen (a common instant reaction); fear of not being perfect in every undertaking, however trivial. All are momentary flashes of fear so ordinary and accustomed that we accept them as normal. But their continuous presence keeps us from experiencing the confident, happy, relaxed state of mind that reflects true potency.

You may ask, if fear exists in virtually everyone, isn't this proof that it is natural and inevitable, even necessary, as a safeguard?

Fear is neither natural nor inevitable. Children reared in families where fear is minimal have markedly different personalities and attitudes from other children. They are more loving, they have sunnier dispositions, they are not worriers, they are more self-reliant, and they do well in whatever pursuits interest them. Moreover, many men and women who have come to adulthood with the usual fear contamination have learned how to eradicate fear and completely change their personalities and their lives.

Another argument against the belief that fear is natural and beneficial is obvious, but generally overlooked. It lies in the assortment of horrors resulting from the combined fears of entire populations. I'm talking about that long, sorry list of deeds of those who control the world's political and financial power, but whose contribution to humanity is nothing to be proud of: wars, territorial disputes, racial and religious conflicts, gigantic military establishments, rapacious corporations, and planet-destroying exploitation of wilderness and resources.

Fear is the energy behind all these ingredients against humanity and against the planet that is our home. We are so accustomed to the erosion of our lives by fear that we tend to shrug off any responsibility for preventing these horrors. When evil comes from masses of people, we are prone to blame human nature. For umpteen generations we have sold ourselves a bill of goods that says "You can't change human nature." It is time to face our responsibilities as adults and acknowledge that social evils are both inhuman and unnatural.

In every situation there is always a choice. We can choose the fear-laden path, or we can express our greatest potential by rejecting fear and dealing directly with the realities of the moment. If we take the latter course, we will have the profound pleasure of solving the problem and increasing our potency at the same time.

5

GROWING UP SCARED

The newborn infant is allowed one act of total, uninhibited freedom. For most human beings it is the last.

Having floated blissfully for months in the perfect environment of the amniotic fluid, the baby suddenly finds its world becoming constrictive and then downright uncomfortable. Forced through the birth canal, it painfully emerges into the world of cool air, bright lights, and loud noises. Terrified and enraged by this change, dangled in space upside down, the infant lets out a howl that is met with complete approval by all present.

The new person has expressed itself with 100 percent potency in reaction to the indignities of entering this world. (Perhaps babies delivered by the LeBoyer method have an easier transition.) Later, it will experience love and pleasure, curiosity and delight, but the first moments hold none of these emotions. Indeed, it is a near miracle that this tiny, helpless creature emotionally survives being born at all!

I wish I could tell every person on this globe never to be afraid of anything. I'd like to say "You successfully lived through the strangest event of your entire life just by being born. Even though you probably cannot remember that experience, nothing you will ever encounter will be so difficult. Take heart! You are stronger than you know. Never be afraid.''

The attack on the infant's potency begins, literally, at the breast. A newborn's most urgently felt need is for food, but even the most willing mother cannot always respond instantly, and the baby feels only its pain and powerlessness. There are other unpleasant sensations that it cannot understand: heat, cold, itching, pain. The baby also knows loneliness. A healthy, wide-awake baby does not like to be left alone in its crib for too long, and will probably cry to be picked up, fondled, and carried to a more interesting environment.

Virtually from the moment of birth, babies receive non-verbal messages that seem to be telling them that they are not welcome and worthy human beings. Such things as tension, hostility, rough handling, or the absence of affectionate physical contact are all sensed by an infant. Thus starts the erosion of potency that, in most cases, will continue for months and years to come.

With so many possibilities of damaging a baby's beautiful, unspoiled nature, are even extremely conscientious parents able to avoid them? I firmly believe they are. It is essential that the child never be demeaned in any way, at any age. The child must receive a continual supply of strokes, assurance, encouragement, praise, and physical affection. A simpler word for all of this is *love*, which includes dignity, respect, understanding, and trust.

Never underestimate the awareness of an infant. A human being is as aware of self at the age of a few months as at thirty years. Those bright eyes staring into ours are perceiving far more than we generally assume. How vital that none of those messages be destructive of the baby's innate potency! At the beginning of life the feeling of self-worth should be scrupulously guarded.

All conscientious parents are caught between what they know and what they feel. During hours of calm, they know all the right ways to handle children. They have read the latest books on child care, they take pride in being modern and progressive, and they declare they will never make the same mistakes their mothers or fathers made with them. But match a father's end-of-the-day fatigue against a little boy's impudent defiance, and the father may react with the same anger his own parent once turned on him.

We parents demean children in so many thoughtless, seemingly insignificant ways, and with such good intentions. We are certain it is our duty to teach them to conform to family values, yet we seldom ask, or even wonder, how a child is feeling at the moment we issue an order.

Children are not horses to be broken. They are as sovereign as adults. Their value as human beings is the equal of their parents'. Only their small size and relative inexperience place children in an inferior position. They are far more intelligent, aware, and capable than most of us perceive—if they are given permission and opportunity to use their abilities unhampered by parental caution and mistrust.

A child's mind is a pristine page waiting to be written upon. So what do we do with this exceptional but fleeting gift of time when a child's mind is growing like a grassy field in spring? Instead of freedom, most families teach fear. They do this, not maliciously, but out of misguided love. The anxious mother overprotects her child because *she* was taught to be afraid. She is fearful and uncomfortable when faced with an unfamiliar situation, never having been encouraged to greet a new challenge with eager anticipation and confidence. Her belief in her abilities is shaky, a fact she's learned to conceal either by being sweet and modest or by reckless bravado. She is usually not aware that it's both desirable and possible to rear a child without the limiting handicap of fear. In fact, she believes that surrounding her child with a blanket of caution and distrust is the best protection she can provide.

I disagree. Fear of any sort is destructive. In a small

child it may set a future pattern of always holding back the natural urge to venture into new endeavors, to risk learning new skills or mastering new fields. The child may also grow up to be different and aloof, hiding behind a protective wall and never knowing true intimacy—a tragic deprivation.

Little children always know what they want. Did you ever see an indecisive baby? Or a two-year-old having a hard time making a choice? They *know*, and they grab for whatever they want with no shilly-shallying. But parents cannot wait to train this remarkable ability out of them. (Years later, these same children will pay money for courses in assertiveness training to learn how to do what they once performed effortlessly.)

A typical child, born innocent and totally natural, finds itself in a household of emotionally contaminated parents, themselves the product of traditional, fear-ridden upbringing. The child expresses a want, then hears "Don't be so selfish! You can't have everything you want!" The child learns fast. It learns what other people say it should want (which provides a solid foundation for later conformity to a materialistic society). On the few occasions when the child gets exactly what it wants, it feels good, happy, self-assured. But if the child persists in asking and is repeatedly refused, it comes to the sad conclusion that the reason is its own unworthiness.

In recent years permissiveness has become a common practice in child-rearing. Seemingly modern and enlightened, it is both destructive and a cop-out. It appeals to couples who are bewildered at the responsibility of dealing with their children, or who fear losing their children's love. Anything goes, until the parents become irritated, at which point they tell the child, "Grow up! Stop being a baby!" A child who hears this message repeatedly may come to believe it is wrong to be a child, and that it is a hindrance and embarrassment to its parents by its very existence.

Children, though intelligent, are not born all-knowing and all-wise. It takes years to acquire sufficient knowledge of the world to live in it safely. One of the chief functions of parents is to provide supportive information that the child has not yet had time or experience to gather. Permissive parents shirk this responsibility.

The Gift of Total Permission

It is possible to give children total permission, which is far different from permissiveness. The permissive parent lets a child do as it pleases, but ignores the child and its actions because of apathy or fear. Permission-giving parents also let a child do as it pleases, because they believe in the child's right to learn by taking charge of its own life—but *only* after giving full information, and then standing by, should the child ask for help.

Permission is one of the most powerful psychic forces. When you are given permission to be intelligent, to be creative, to be unafraid, you are far more likely to be so than if you had to forge ahead on your own. For permission could also be called *encouragement,* or *I believe in you.*

Our children know that we care about them very deeply, they trust and believe us when we give them permission to make mistakes; we tell them that mistakes are a part of learning and not the horrendous evil generally supposed. We also give them permission to actualize themselves: to tackle new projects, learn new skills, meet new and different people, and be unafraid of failing. If they do "fail," they know that is all right, too. From the time when our youngest child was six, and we changed from being traditional parents to permission-giving parents, all the boys have been responsible for their own decisions and actions. We give them guidance, but we both want and encourage them to do as they please.

However, they are not turned loose to flounder blindly in ignorance. They have received much practical information, though not in an authoritarian, threatening, or restrictive way. For although each is free to do whatever, in his own judgement, he feels is best, we make sure he is aware of other alternatives and any hazards surrounding his choice. Our sons know society punishes nonconformists, even though their parents do not. We don't force them to attend school, but so far none have dropped out. One boy decided that school was too boring to attend, and stayed out a week or two. When the truant officer called me, I told him it was not my affair and turned the astonished man over to my son. They settled the matter between them and my son decided to return to school.

For years our sons have called us Helen and Stan, not Mom and Dad. There is enormous sentimentality and hypocrisy built up around the latter words. Two hundred years ago, European and American children were calling their fathers *Sir*, a title symbolic of the tyrannical power fathers then held over their helpless and fearful offspring. (Many wives, for that matter, called their husbands *Mister*.) We have come a long way since then; Mom and Dad are vast improvements over Ma'am and Sir, but they are still tainted relics of traditional inequality between young and old.

Formality of any sort is a barricade to intimacy, that highest, most beautiful state of human relations. Parents who are afraid they will lose their children's respect if they allow lines of authority to break down, or who insist upon unquestioning obedience, are parents destined to future sorrow and disappointment.

Our relationship with our sons is based on a firm, yet essentially uncomplicated, philosophy. It is this: *We do not own our children.* They have been entrusted to our care for the youthful period of their lives, but not their adult lives. We will not, as so many parents do, treat them as children even when they themselves are parents and middle-aged. Indeed, we do not treat them as incompetent "children" even now, by patronizing and talking down to them.

We have their respect because we respect them, for respect is a mutual affair. We consider them as priceless and irreplaceable as if they were one-of-a-kind art objects put in our hands to safeguard and preserve for posterity.

In essence, we will not violate our children's sovereignty. By sovereignty, I mean that invisible psychic, emotional, mental, legal, and sometimes physical space around each human being which belongs to each of us alone. Sovereignty is the basic right to be independent of outside intrusion, and to be autonomous in deciding what *we* judge right for *us* to do—in simple words: our total, separate individuality.

Parents who accept the reality that children will usually not behave like adults, and are prepared to cope with each situation without feeling the child is personally combative, are one jump ahead of the game. These parents know that children will break things, get dirty, tear their clothes, lose their caps and mittens, and knock over their glasses of milk. The old saw, "Don't cry over spilled milk" should have a second meaning: "Don't scold your kid when he spills it!"

These parents will also do their best to anticipate trouble before it becomes an emergency. They will explain in quiet interludes that sharp knives can cut, fire can burn, electricity can shock, etc., not in fear-producing dramatics, but in a way that lets the child know the parents respect its intelligence. For children *are* intelligent, and their intelligence expands with each adult acknowledgment of its existence. In real emergencies, of course, one must act peremptorily, and later explain to the child with love and patience.

Rearing children is not a bed of roses, even though popular fancy would have you think so. Romanticism and sentimentality surround the myth: Birth announcement cards depict angelic cherubs, innocent little lambs who have dropped from heaven to brighten our lives. Well, they do brighten them, most of the time, but they can also infuriate. Children are not innocent. Nobody is. Innocence is a myth; the correct word is *ignorance*. In a child this is not a fault, but a vacuum that parents have the responsibility to fill with information, for an ignorant child is a vulnerable child, unequipped for the world. The informed child is not restricted to one course of action; it has many options from which to make a personally suitable choice.

Childhood is the time for children to use their imaginations and to feel their emotions, including all the painful ones. Let them feel their jealousies, fears, and anger. Parents should not force children to repress these natural emotions. What children *do* with an emotion is supremely important: whether it is turned into violence against themselves or others or into rational thinking, and parents can help them see the difference. Childhood is the time when the emotional patterns of life are established.

We would all like to surround our children with so much love that the world could never harm them. This is, of course, impossible, and parents who try to do it actually harm their loved ones. Children who are overprotected are like fawns raised in captivity, then turned loose in the wilderness with no knowledge of how to survive. Let your child *experience* its life. Let the child literally and figuratively fall down. Let it get muddy. But *be there*, and if it asks you to wipe off the mud and kiss the hurt, do so without lecturing, or forcing either cleanliness or kisses! Nothing you say could compare with what it learns from its own pain. Most of all, let your child know that she or he is loved by you—no matter what.

6

STILL SCARED

Our tradition-bound universities are fine training grounds for fear. Here are trained the nation's future leaders of business, industry, communication, transportation, government, science, and the professions. The word *train* is precise because of its connotation of mastering a prescribed program and never deviating from it. University graduates are not being educated, in the finest sense, but they are being well-trained. They learn, through subtle and not so subtle pressures, that natural curiosity and creativity are best subordinated to pleasing professors and gaining a degree.

By the time they enter college, students are already well on their way to conforming to the standard fears of society. It is not enough that they conform to society's goals. They must conform to its fears as well: the fear of failure, the fear of being left behind by competitors, the fear of not accumulating enough money, the fear of not knowing the "right" behavior. In essence it has become fearful to be an outsider.

Follow with me, one bright autumn morning, a young man about to set off on a momentous day, his first in college. One intense worry is behind him; Ed has survived the competition for admittance. During his senior high school year, he had tortured himself with negative fantasies of being turned down by this university, his father's Alma Mater.

The campus of the University of Americana is imposing. Built years ago, when state money flowed freely, its pseudo-Gothic structures and spacious, tree-dotted lawns successfully convey their message: "This is the Established Way; here you will learn what wiser men than you have written. We do not expect you to rise to their level, for they were geniuses, not ordinary mortals. We only ask that you absorb, memorize, and regurgitate what they passed down to you, or it's Out, boy, Out! Don't ever forget: This university has no room for failures—or radical thinkers!"

On the first day of classes Ed muddles through by perseverance, choking down a continuous procession of fears. Poring anxiously over a campus map, he ultimately finds his way through the maze of paths to the right building. Finding a seat, he casts timid glances at the other students. After his nonchalant high school days, where he was one of the elite, this first session of his first university class sends a chill through his body.

The professor, unlit pipe in hand, stands before the class and casts a look of weary boredom and sardonic amusement at the new recruits. The roomful of students is cowed into sober silence; this guy will be no cinch. Ed wishes for one wild moment that he could run away, anything but stay in this classroom, with this frightening ogre who controls his future. But a greater fear, the fear of making a fool of himself, holds Ed fast in his seat. That fear is reinforced by another lesson he learned well long before, the lesson of conformity. We do not do the unusual, we do only what is expected. Therein lies "safety."

Ed is bright, so he learns quickly how to survive. He learns to stifle the innovative ideas that sometimes occur to him, for after a few attempts, he found that they only provoked arguments, and poor grades. Since high grades are essential to achieving a degree, Ed abandons his own ideas. He has almost forgotten the thrilling notions he held in the summer between high school and college, when he planned to change the world somehow, make it a better place. In his senior year he can smile as condescendingly at the green frosh as his first professor did.

Ed realizes now that a Bachelor's degree won't take him far in the business world, with the competition from a thousand others bearing the same useless initials after their names. So he plods up the slopes of Academe, passes the minor peak of Master, and finally reaches that Everest, a Ph.D.

Harmony Corporation hires Ed, and for a time he basks in a glow of self-satisfaction. As he begins to learn Harmony's rigid structure, however, he becomes aware that he is at the bottom of the corporate ladder, with a hundred other brighter, more experienced men solidly blocking his upward climb. Not to mention the dozens of entry-level Ph.D's all shrewdly maneuvering to beat each other to the first empty foothold one rung up!

Fear sets in again, stronger this time. Ed is in his thirties now; he has lost some of his youthful optimism, he has a wife and son to support, and an image of success to maintain. His present struggle is for keeps. He can't possibly back out now. He has invested too much time, money, and emotional energy in his profession to think of dropping out. Besides, what would people think?

He tells no one of his fear that he is locked into a dead end from which, even by intensely competitive labor, he doesn't have the brains or stamina to dislodge himself. A recurring pain in his stomach is diagnosed as an ulcer. Still Ed struggles on, swallowing his fear (and pills for the ulcer), working long hours, bringing work home night after night, to the annoyance of his wife. He wishes he had time to see more of his son, but knows it is more important to succeed on the job. After all, he wants to send *his* kid to college, just as he and his father were sent.

Ed's wife Jill has traveled a path different from Ed's, for she is female, but it is just as stereotyped, and has left her just as confused about her real nature as he is about his own. They met, fell in love and married while Jill was still an undergraduate. With funds sufficient for only one student, there was no question as to which one should continue. Jill, following tradition, dropped out gracefully and got a job. Women are supposed to step back in favor of men when there isn't enough of something to go around. In addition, Jill was expected to feel a strong nesting urge and to enjoy keeping house in the hours left over from the job.

Ed and Jill faithfully adhered to their separate cultural scripts. Ed spent all day and evening at his studies, which were more important than either of Jill's two occupations. If Jill ever grew physically tired, she felt guilty at not being a better manager.

Not until many years later does Jill begin to wonder why she feels vaguely troubled and suffers mysterious ailments the doctors assure her are "all in the head." She sees that somehow, despite all her uncomplaining cooperation, the reward of a companionable family life has been denied her. She sacrificed *her* chance to develop her potentials so that Ed might have his chance. Yet what good was it, after all? Her husband is a slave to a corporation, a silent man at home, his head buried in a briefcase. For all his degrees, he seems no happier than she. Even their infrequent sexual encounters are disappointing and lack the fire of their early love. After years of dutifully subordinating her own interests to her husband's welfare, and actually suppressing her personality until it became a shadowy reflection of his, Jill wakes to a bitter sense of having been cheated all along.

Picture, then, this family of three: middle-class, attractive, intelligent, and prosperous. You would assume they possess all anyone could desire. Now eavesdrop on their thoughts.

Ed is saying to himself:

- I work hard for you and our son, but you don't appreciate it.
- I feel you don't love me and I'm afraid to approach you sexually.
- I feel lost as a parent; my son seems afraid of me.
- I feel I'll never go higher on the job.
- I wonder why I failed. Should I have chosen another field?
- I wonder what people think of me.
- I'm getting old. What's ahead, if anything?

Jill thinks:

- I don't want you to work so hard because I want your companionship.
- I feel you don't love me any more. The only time you pretend to is when you want sex, so I don't respond.
- I didn't resent working to help you through college, but now I do resent missing my chance.
- I resent being stuck with housework when I was doing two jobs! You still don't appreciate me.
- Sometimes I think of leaving you but I'm afraid of what people would say, and I'm afraid of trying something new.

(Notice how Jill's thoughts still focus on Ed rather than herself.)

Their son says:

- My dad never takes me anywhere.
- He doesn't want me to bother him. I have to be quiet and stay away.
- I don't know why my mother is so crabby and strict.
- I'll be glad when I grow up!

If only they dared to speak their thoughts aloud! Expecting another person to be a mind-reader is self-destructive.

Keeping silent does not make hurt feelings go away; they continue to smoulder until one day they are beyond control. Then anger and violence may destroy what might have been saved.

What Ed and Jill can't see, because they are so fearful, is that their lives are not set in concrete! *Options are open to them.* No legal statute says that Ed must remain in his job or that Jill must be an unappreciated domestic worker. Their twelve-year-old son has fewer options. He can run away, and some his age have survived this drastic choice, but he deserves a better future. Meantime he can only go on hoping for a change in his parents' behavior, or wait until he is old enough to be independent.

Ed, Jill and their son can sit down together, possibly with a professional, or even a trusted mutual friend, and voice their worries. Once the first halting statements are spoken, the rest will come rushing out. They will probably discover that instead of being poles apart, their desires and dissatisfactions are very similar. They can explore the multitude of options open to them when they allow their creative, positive fantasies expression.

No idea, however wild and foolish, need be dismissed. They can tell each other what mad adventure each has always dreamed of—then figure out how to pursue it in the year ahead. A plan does not have to be perfect before being tried. A plan has a life of its own, changing and growing like a sprouting seed.

The son will undoubtedly demand to be a voting member of the family, and their stereotyped roles will change, moving towards equality and cooperation. Ed may opt to start his own business; Jill may choose to return to college. Or all three may decide to kick over the traces, buy a boat and vagabond around the world! No matter if eventually any plan runs its course and is abandoned, it won't be a failure unless they choose to call it so. It will be an expression of aliveness, of actualizing themselves, and of creating and following positive fantasies.

What's the gamble? Aren't the risks higher when a miserable existence leads only to death?

The family message repeated around the globe is the same, generation after generation. By contrast, government systems have changed as people devised new ways to wrest power from the elite. Feudalism, church rule, and monarchies had their day. Technology evolved from primitive tools and the discovery of fire to animal power, sail, steam, petroleum, electricity, and nuclear and solar energy. Each change eventually met with nearly universal acceptance and praise. Why, then, has the rearing of each new generation changed so little from ancient times to the present? In all societies, the customs and beliefs of the adult generation have been poured into the consciousness of that most pliable and receptive vessel, a young child's mind.

No doubt it is this very pliability that has perpetuated family tradition. Cultural and family attitudes and customs are almost purely emotional. The ways of the family and the culture are impressed upon the child's mind daily, as much a part of its existence as food. Family traditions are *ingrained* in the child's whole being; to change them is almost as impossible as to change the color of its eyes.

What are the characteristics of family tradition? Details differ around the globe, but two elements are constant: power and fear. Power is the universal force that shapes the family structure. This kind of power is not potency. This power is authority, not over oneself, but over others. It may be kindly or harsh, but is respected by those upon whom it is exercised. In a subtle way, this power is turned over freely by the very ones subjugated to it.

Traditionally, the father possesses the power in the family. Generally physically stronger and larger than the female, the male assumed the power in primitive societies where those characteristics were at a premium, and there has been little challenge of that power until recently.

Consequently father, primitive or civilized, has been

the master of the family and laid down its laws, many of which derive from the ancient lore he absorbed as a child. The mother accepts his dominant position unquestioningly, or with concealed objections, the children may grumble and rebel, but their rebellion seldom succeeds.

The other element common to family structures is fear. Fear is the emotion which supports and maintains power. Without fear, power would collapse!

Why does a child or a wife obey (thus giving power to) the father/husband? Essentially because of fear. The child knows that disobedience will bring punishment, physical or verbal, and has learned to fear pain and humiliation. The fear may be an everyday sensation, but it affects the child in many insidious ways and causes the loss of potency.

Why is the wife afraid? She would probably deny her fear indignantly; yet under all is a real fear of upsetting her marriage if she doesn't cater to her husband's wishes, and of losing him to another, more subservient, woman. Many women will defer to their husbands at all costs to maintain harmony in the home. At all costs—what irony! For the cost to both of them is high. She loses some of her integrity and becomes less potent. He gains power, but loses real potency.

I don't want to give the impression that what ails today's family is the fault of men. Men are as much the victims of blind tradition as women. Each has learned from the cradle what his or her role is to be, and each is rewarded for faithful adherence to that role.

If you believe that this is no longer true in our enlightened age, then picture a family where the wife works as a telephone installer and the husband stays home to care for the house and children. No good reason exists why this should not be satisfactory to all concerned, but it takes a brave couple to carry it out. Our society sees the husband as stepping down in life, and is critical of his wife for seeming to "wear the pants" in the family.

Is the power of tradition, a power based on fear, too sacred to be subjected to intelligent scrutiny? Of course not. It is high time that we overhaul our primitive ideas of family relations. The family can and should be a place wherein each member is able to find the greatest possible fulfillment of abilities and desires. Reclaiming our power for ourselves and supporting other family members to do the same is all that is required.

7

WINNING THE MATING GAME

Infants are born without sexual preferences. A baby girl does not exclusively prefer males, nor a baby boy, females. They respond with pleasure and affection to anybody who treats them well. Until babies learn through sad experience to fear persons or things, they actually like everyone and everything!

If reared in a family where love and kindness are the rule, the young child will shower its love on all persons, regardless of sex. It knows no inhibitions, and will touch and explore any part of its own body or those around it. The toddler, long since weaned, will still try to reach its mother's breast because it feels good. The baby will also explore its father's body, for at this age the sex of the parent means nothing.

By the time of entering first grade, however, the child knows that all of humankind is split into two extremely different halves, male and female. Children, contrary to most parents' beliefs, are intensely interested in sex. They might be just as curious about hamburgers and french fries if they had never seen or tasted them, yet they suspected their existence through smirking references and incomprehensible jokes—especially if questions brought only evasive answers, or even reprimands. Nothing shines a brighter spotlight on something hidden than to call it wicked and taboo. Aside from parental mystification of the subject, however, children do have a natural interest in their bodies and their sexuality, just as they are interested in everything about themselves and the world around them. They are naturally sexual, which I call naturosexual.

But with boys and girls trained from infancy into separate sexual stereotypes (guns and trucks, dolls and dishes), the two sexes learn to play and develop apart. Watch a school playground; seldom will you see a mixed game or group. Children who formerly played together with little awareness of sex differences now separate themselves, or are separated by adults, into two groups with less and less in common. Each sex absorbs daily, by instruction or example, what is expected of it.

As the sexes grow up with ever diverging goals, their studies and play reinforcing these goals, males and females become unfathomable mysteries to each other. Men often say "I don't understand women!" and women find men equally incomprehensible. Neither sex experiences this degree of bafflement with members of their own sex, however. In each sex there also seems to exist an unspoken, almost unconscious, allegiance that surfaces on occasion against the other sex in general, regardless of an individual's feelings for a particular member of the other sex. Before looking at the traditional heterosexual marriage relationship, let us take a look at those who have followed nontraditional paths, sometimes at considerable cost to themselves.

Homosexuality

In contrast to the uncertainty and fear felt by each sex toward the other, the comfortable familiarity between members of the same sex is a strong incentive to love someone of one's own sex. Though sexual activity among children and adolescents may be prohibited by parents, curiosity regarding sex is too strong in young people to postpone by mere injunction. In addition to the fact that the human mind at any age is clever at devising ways to conceal unauthorized acts, more opportunities for homosexual experimentation between young people exist because the same sexes routinely associate together. The alarm signals that ring out in a parent's brain when a daughter shows an interest in a young man are usually silent when her new friend is another girl (and vice versa, with a son). It is known that many youngsters have some same-sex experience in early maturation, although most later become exclusively heterosexual.

For those whose lifetime sexual orientation is homosexual, however, society reserves its greatest disapproval. Even murder and war are considered more acceptable. Yet look at the subject coolly for a moment, setting societal prejudices aside temporarily. This sexual preference, except for the guilt and fear instilled by traditional mores, is a pleasurable, loving, and joyous state of being when experienced by those who prefer it.

Lovers of the same sex have the same intense feelings that any male-female couple experience when they fall in love. They are likely to have the same clashes of opinion and personality and the resulting quarrels. There is absolutely no difference in their feelings for one another. The homosexual couple cannot procreate, but neither can infertile heterosexual couples.

Occasionally a person who had homosexual relationships during youth, but later married, will look back at those experiences and decide that they provided a fuller measure of happiness than the present marriage, and will then return to a permanent, exclusively homosexual way of life. The decisions of such persons, who have tested both worlds, should at the least give one pause to reconsider one's own rigid convictions.

Love—any expression of love—in a world so full of hate should be welcomed with rejoicing. Gay people have the same aspirations for a happy life as straight people. They laugh and cry and worry, get sick, get well, have accidents and recover, work and go to school, succeed and fail, just like everyone else. Some have children from previous heterosexual marriages whom they care for as deeply—or as indifferently—as the straights. The sole difference is that they happen to love persons of the same sex. For that they are reviled and ostracized from society, mainly because of society's unreasoning fear of something of which it has no understanding.

Bisexuality

This choice in human relationships, because it excludes neither sex as a source of love and companionship, offers those who adopt it twice the potential for understanding, growth, and participation in the lives of others. Its rewards are an expanding of mental and emotional horizons and a greater life enrichment, but its demands are also high. Few people are ready or willing to take the risks involved, and there are many. Long-held beliefs must be re-evaluated before undertaking this mode of life, and one must consider the pressures of society in general as well as the difficulties raised by one's immediate circle of family and associates.

The internal challenge is unquestionably the greater. Before an individual can feel at ease in adopting bisexuality, he or she must first have peeled off all the layers of stereotypical attitudes wrapped around the natural mind and feelings. There must be a return to that idyllic state of consciousness of the small child before it learned to fear and distrust, when it felt only love and boundless zest for all the wonders of the world around it, including all human individuals, whom it loved without regard for their sex. Naturosexuality!

Obviously this emotional transformation is extremely difficult, and probably seldom achieved completely in our Western world. But it is a transformation to aspire to, whatever mode of sexual behavior one chooses. Unlike the infant, the adult possesses a vast store of experience and the capacity to reason; these must somehow be coordinated with the adult's newfound naturalness. Accomplishing this is not easy; it takes time and dedication, but it has been done.

Bisexual people find themselves in an oddly unprotected position, exposed and vulnerable on all sides to the onslaughts of other attitudes and beliefs. Lacking the security of the heterosexual, and rejected by many who are solely homosexual, the bisexual has neither the sanctioned position in society of the former, nor, tenuous though it is, the refuge and mutual support afforded by the gay subculture.

In a few parts of the world (like San Francisco, Berkeley, Paris, London, or New York), where an intellectual climate has allowed a certain freedom of thought and exploration of new solutions to old problems of living, the bisexual person may find a coterie of like-minded individuals from whom to draw support for unconventional beliefs. Elsewhere the person who has the capacity freely to love all of humanity must face hatred and shocked disapproval from most of them.

Community Living

Creative fantasies are emerging frequently these days as people use their ingenuity in seeking new ways to deal with the eternal quest for human companionship. Two experiments, both of which have economic incentives as well, are communes and intentional communities.

Communes are usually formed by groups of young people (and sometimes older ones) with similar philosophies who wish to join forces and live together, with varying degrees of separation from the outside world. Some choose a large house in a city, where they set up a family government for maintaining harmony while still encouraging individual autonomy. Outside jobs are held as needed or desired, and household work and expenses shared by all, men and women. Sexual relationships may or may not be shared outside primary relationships, but advance agreement on this matter is usually a requisite for joining the commune.

Similar communes are formed in rural or wilderness areas by those renouncing materialism and artificiality for a more basic, earthy existence. Their social framework may vary widely from group to group, but like the city commune they are based on strong ties and allegiance to the group.

Intentional communities are usually larger and composed of monogamous couples, married or unmarried, with similar creative interests, who join together for economic reasons and also for mutual help and inspiration in their professions. One such group lives in Chicago during the winter, then spends summers farming in Michigan, an arrangement that many tradition-bound city workers with only two-week yearly vacations might well envy.

These departures from traditional living have their successes and failures like all human ventures. But they are tangible proof that more and more people are dissatisfied with the old, traditional way to live a life, and they are willing to take the risks in finding a better way.

What Price Matrimony?

The majority of people still marry and hope for the best, even though they know that half the marriages today end

in divorce. Despite increasing demand for equality between the sexes (for men as well as for women), most
young people pay this concept lip service only. They are
often unaware of the subtle manifestations of inequality
that surround them until they show up glaringly in a traditional marriage relationship.

The young man who was fascinated by his fiancee's
flippant, charming unconventionality, her dancing skills,
and her success in a job is inevitably disappointed and
then resentful if after the wedding she turns out to be a
poor cook and housekeeper. He envies her supposed freedom and leisure at home while he battles the tough world
outside. When children come along, he is, perhaps unconsciously, jealous of her attentions to them and manifests
that feeling by issuing harsh orders to both children and
wife. He despairs at the mounting financial demands of
the enlarging family, and looks back wistfully at his care-
free bachelor days. He begins to feel trapped in a lifetime
of obligations. Yet, well-trained, he does not express these
thoughts in a forthright way. Instead, he may become bitter and sarcastic or retreat into taciturn resignation.
Whichever road he chooses to follow, the man has surrendered much of his original potency to the marriage myth,
and his chances for fulfilling himself have all but vanished.

How does the woman, who he feels has the better part
of the bargain, regard *her* situation? She may now be the
homemaker her husband hoped for, but she experiences
growing boredom at the identical tasks she must perform
each day. She fears her mind is vegetating and dreams of
the job she used to have. Her girlhood held out the goal of
marriage and happily-ever-after. Now, still half-believing
in that marriage/happiness myth, she wonders: Where did
I go wrong? Why did I imagine him to be so different from
what he really is? Her husband becomes jealous if she ap-
pears to enjoy another man's company, but she wonders if
he takes his secretary to lunch.

This couple is the victim of traditional marriage. Both husband and wife accepted without question their sexually stereotyped roles. Later, neither revealed their bewilderment and hurt because they were not brought up to be open and candid. Expert deceivers by the time they reached marriage, both spouses camouflaged their real dissatisfactions by raging at trivial incidents instead.

Transactional Analysis calls this game-playing. In a world where honest expression of feelings is socially incorrect, learning and using games are a method of survival. Unfortunately, in the long run they don't work. Game-playing causes misunderstanding, resentment, and, worst of all, the erosion of personal potency.

Ideal Marriage

Unlike traditional marriage, the ideal marriage is a union of two individuals who are already whole, possessed of their full potency, and uncontaminated by false standards and stereotypical attitudes. They are not two incomplete persons who hope by marrying to become whole, each propping the other up. The romantic myth is that each complements the other, the failing in one made up by the strengths of the other. The reality is that one person, usually the woman, becomes subservient to the other.

An ideal marriage allows both partners and their children the freedom to grow. The intermingling relationships among the members of the family will become deeper and dearer, but never rigid and demanding. Family ties will be strong and resilient, always stretching in infinite lines of love and support.

Ideal marriages are rare, however, because fully potent people are rare in our culture. Even such marriages have their limitations. The human race is composed of a broad spectrum of individuals with different tastes, personalities, talents, education, upbringing, experience, racial and national origins, chronological age, and physical appearance. These variations make life interesting, and no one person can ever possess them all! Thus a man and a woman in a closed, monogamous relationship may one day awake to an uneasy boredom and a feeling that life and all its unfulfilled promises are passing them by. They still love each other, but there is a *sameness* in living that nags them.

At this dull plateau in their lives one of the pair may secretly take a lover. The excitement of a new love and the feeling that life has suddenly acquired a thrilling new dimension may be satisfying at first, but eventually guilt and the fear of discovery outweighs euphoria, and when inevitably the mate learns the unwelcome truth, the result is anger and confused remorse.

Trying to combine personal sexual freedom and a traditional marriage *simply doesn't work.* Each person in the eternal triangle suffers: the innocent mate feels betrayed, the straying mate feels guilty and torn between two loves, and the third party feels exploited and lonely. These unhappy consequences are well-known. Fear of losing the mate and fear of social condemnation deter many who are attracted to someone outside a marriage, but the fear does not remove their longing. Either way they are unhappy and perplexed after condemning themselves for wanting to disobey time-honored rules of behavior.

It is hard to trust your own feelings when all of society says they are wrong, but I am convinced that conformity to popular beliefs runs counter to human needs. Though once a true conformist myself, I gradually realized that the source of most emotional problems is the disparity between society's rules and people's natural longing for a wider, deeper experience of life in their brief time on earth.

Out of those years of often painful introspection, I have

evolved my own personal philosophy. It is nonconforming, not because I *want* to defy convention, but because it is necessary. Establishment rules are destructive of the human spirit; they suffocate growth and produce miserable lives.

My credo is simple, but strong: *I am in charge of my own life.* For that, I must be free to make my own decisions, expand my own horizons. I must be completely honest in all my contacts with others, I must avoid secrecy, and *I must never violate another's sovereignty.* Human transactions are a two-way street, and I respect the interests and well-being of others equally with my own.

Opening a Marriage

A married person in our society, who sees its tyranny over people's lives and decides to stop being its victim while there is still time to discover life's potentials, faces a formidable dilemma.

It is never easy to tell your astonished mate that, although you still love her or him, you feel stifled, disappointed, worried, confused, and scared, while at the same time you are determined to create a better life for both of you.

Once you have broken the ice, though, you will pour out your conviction that this marriage is crippling you both, that playing the roles of superboss, breadwinner husband, and doting, house-drudge wife, is not a splendid way to live a life. You will pour out your craving to feel alive again, to choose to do something, anything, on your own as a *separate individual*, with no one cluck-clucking or frowning.

You tell him or her that you want the freedom to grow, that you want to make new friends of both sexes, and that you may even find another sexual partner. You earnestly reassert that you love your mate and do not wish to break up the marriage but only to open its locked doors and shove out its confining walls.

If at this point the response is a sarcastic comment about "having your cake and eating it, too," you might reply "Why not? What are the rewards of self-denial and self-sacrifice except a narrow, impoverished existence?" But your mate may surprise you and own up to having felt similar longings that were quickly suppressed. If so, you are both fortunate and your paths will be smoother.

Opening up a restrictive marriage can be as varied as the people involved. It is a new experience for everyone and, as I like to remind people faced with any kind of change, "There are no rules for jumping into the New, for no one has ever been there before!" Your experience, my experience, and the other fellow's will all be different, just as we are all different from each other. The basic ingredients for a successful open marriage are honest communication and trust between the original primary partners *(including their children)* and all other persons involved. In this respect, the fundamental requirements for a workable open marriage do not differ from the trust and honesty essential to any other satisfactory human encounter.

Contrary to the usual assumption, an open marriage does not necessarily include outside sexual relationships. There are hundreds of ways to enlarge one's life besides the sexual, and many people will prefer other choices. A basic premise of an open marriage (or open relationship, for this discussion pertains to any couple living together, married or not) is that each partner freely grants the other an agreed-upon amount of time in which to follow his or her own pursuits. Because each partner gives consent (permission), no sense of guilt or selfishness remains to cloud the full enjoyment of private time. This is not a trivial point; the fact of mutual agreement and permission between both partners is the very heart of a successful open relationship.

Asking for or giving permission for outside sexual activity is, no doubt about it, the most difficult step of all. A curious fact often emerges: Although a partner may believe in an open relationship for himself or herself, and may have one or more lovers, it may cause intense worry and fear when the mate does the same.

A longtime closed relationship, even though it seems to be functioning well, may actually improve after opening. Many couples say they would never return to the marriage they once had because their lives have become incredibly full and joyous. The most unforeseen outcome frequently is that the love and attraction between the original two increases beyond their wildest imaginings.

It must be noted that open relationships do not always succeed. In fact, they probably have as many failures as traditional marriage. People may plunge in with unrealistic expectations, without clearly understanding that they may not demand more privileges than they are willing to grant, forgetting that inequality of rights and obligations is what created the need for openness in the first place. Or they may fail because no plan for negotiating disputes is set up before trouble erupts. Open relationships may fail for many of the same reasons that closed, traditional ones fail—arguments over money, duties, and promises; jealousy and fear of losing one's partner, or even boredom and incompatibility of interests.

But the main cause of failure is lack of outside support: from friends, relatives, associates, churches, organizations, television, the press, our entire culture. Even therapists and psychologists, supposedly sources of help, are often negative. The practice of open marriage, while it has existed to a limited degree in one form or another down through history, is still an unknown quantity to most people. Their initial reaction, therefore, is to resent and fear it as a threat to their own entrenched beliefs.

The best way to get support if you are a believer in open relationships is to create a support group yourself. By meeting together regularly, all the members will have a source of help to turn to when personal problems arise, or when outside pressures become intolerable. Having a skilled leader is an excellent arrangement, but even without one, airing problems and receiving encouragement and suggestions from understanding friends will usually be sufficient support. Finding others in open relationships may not be easy, depending on where you live and the local climate toward such a philosophy. You'll need to draw on your power of creative fantasy. And don't forget the power of advertising.

Attempting to go it alone is to attempt to fight the army of ignorance singlehandedly. Strength, as always, lies in union, which is the source of those three important P's so essential to your well-being: permission, protection, and potency.

Until you become stronger and can give them to yourself, the first two will come from group members. Their permission means their approval of you and your beliefs and way of life. This is extremely important; without approval from *someone* most people could not survive emotionally.

The second essential, protection, also comes from the group, and at times from individual members as well. You may need protection from criticism by neighbors or the community, or protection from your own occasional negative feelings. Being able to phone a friend at the very moment of need can be crucial, and communication between group members at any hour of the day or night is encouraged.

The third essential, potency, in spirit and actions, will be the reward you give yourself as a result of group support and your own resulting growth in self-esteem.

Benefits of Open Marriage

Is an open relationship worth the risk? No human activity is without risk; it is the unfamiliar risk that is fearful. People continually gamble with traditional marriage because it is the familiar custom, even though they know that half are destined to lose by divorce, and many others will lose in less obvious ways.

The concept of marriage is one of our greatest illusions. There *is no such thing as a marriage*. It is a fantasy created by two individuals who say they are married. They repeat certain words before a clergyman, and— presto!—they step into a space called marriage, which they believe transforms them into new and different human beings. The awesome power of fantasy! For nothing is changed; they are the same persons they were before, unsure, concealing their fears, but hoping marriage will change all that. If it doesn't, many will run pell-mell into a second traditional marriage, convinced that the failure of the first was due only to a wrong choice of partner.

Some thoughtful souls caught twice in the same trap will begin to examine their predicament and reject the old cliches. After a great deal of thought and discussion, they may decide that opening their marriage, breaking out its smothering walls, and stepping out of their own stifling roles is their only hope. They know that this new way of life will bring its own brand of problems, but that their solution won't be linked to conformity with rules imposed by society. Rather, it will depend upon their own free and honest creative intelligence.

Society is full of lies; one is the myth that almost every young person believes: "Get married and live happily every after." This disillusioned couple knows better, and they refuse to sacrifice themselves merely because some indeterminate "they" say they must. Such people do not deserve the condemnation of society; they have almost all tried very hard to live by its dictates, but found them wanting.

In their new, opened relationship they discover a heightened awareness of life in general. This state of consciousness does not emerge immediately; radical changes in attitudes and lifestyle take time to assimilate. But after they have become familiar and no longer frightening, most persons experience an increased enjoyment of everything—of people, activities, and environment, and most surprising and welcome of all, a higher level of self-esteem.

Deciding Not to Forsake All Others

In professional work with groups, large workshops, and in question-and-answer sessions after lectures, I have heard enthusiastic reports from many who have adopted an open lifestyle for one, five, ten or more years, but the one I know best is my own.

My wife Helen and I were aware a number of years ago that open marriage existed; we thought it a theoretically interesting development but held no firm views on it, pro or con, nor did we consider it applicable to us. Then one day I received a letter from a woman listener to my radio program at WLS in Chicago:

Oct. 12, 1970

Dear Stan:

I want to share our personal marital philosophy with you and perhaps your listeners. Although we've never discussed it with other people, I suppose it is unusual.

We were married at 19 and 21, eleven years ago. We fortunately have always kept open our lines of communication, and have grown in the same direction together. Our marriage has been further strengthened by our love for our two daughters, six and eight, and watching them grow into independent, joyful little individuals. Our family solidarity is structured on open and honest communion with each other. Our entire relationship, sexual and otherwise, becomes more enchanting year after year!

We believe the reason for our happiness is that we have never, never tried to own or possess each other. We respect each other's privacy and treasure our own and the other's individuality and independence. This concept is unspoken and unstructured—it just has always been that way. Our love for each other and for our children has never been a smothering, destructive force, and is based on our innate respect for each other. We project the same respect in our thoughts about all human beings, and hope we are encouraging our daughters to do the same.

One big reason we dig each other so much is that we both reach out to other people, realizing that most of life is learning from, living in harmony with, and loving other people. If we cut ourselves off from relating to beautiful people, and some not so beautiful, and kept relationships on a superficial level, what uninteresting, unenriched, dulled spirits we'd bring to each other and our children! If we depended entirely on our own closeness, what would we be if something suddenly happened to one of us and the other was left alone?

There's no spoken agreement about sexual relationships with others, but we impose no limits on each other in our development of friendships outside our marriage. We are not promiscuous swingers, but feel that sex is often a part of developing meaningful, responsive human interchange. We believe touching and physical awareness are natural facets of many healthy alliances between people. Often it isn't necessary, but if sex is required and will help fulfill a relationship, it is not wrong. We don't guiltily think, "I can't; it's off limits because I'm married." In its own special context it is completely detached from our marriage, but if a conflict arose in our minds we would know it was hurtful to ourselves and to each other, and we would not continue with it.

We believe the capacity to give and receive love is virtually limitless. We would not warp ourselves, and each other, by saying, "You must channel *all* of yourself to me, and *only* me, *all* of the time!" Instead, we must develop ourselves and life every moment as fully as possible, bringing to our marriage all the enrichment and fulfillment we acquire along the way. What greater gift could we give each other? Certainly, exclusivity of minds and bodies uninfluenced by the intelligence, warmth, and beauty of other people cannot match the exchange we have.

It is hard to verbalize these feelings, but I hope this presents some idea of the beauty in our kind of marriage.

Sincerely,

This woman was saying what I had been feeling subliminally. For years, my work in radio interviewing had brought me in touch with many interesting people, both men and women. Often I wished to continue their acquaintance after the broadcast, and would go to coffee or dinner with the men, but never with the women! That was verboten according to society's rules, which I followed dutifully. What would Helen think if I took a beautiful movie star to dinner?

The letter made sense, not only to my wife and me, but also to thousands who requested copies after I read it on the air. As single persons, it had been quite proper for both Helen and me to make as many new friends of the other sex as we liked. If becoming married automatically cut off those contacts, actually shrank our lives instead of expanding them, then there must be something wrong.

We had considered our marriage a happy one, until we both began to bring our feelings out into the light of day. Then we became aware that each had buried many a desire for occasional privacy, or freedom to go somewhere or do something on our own without feeling duty-bound to ask permission first, or to at least inform the other. It dawned on us that the typical married person exchanges one set of masters, his or her parents, for another, the spouse and children! Attaining adulthood did not bestow freedom to experience one's own individuality, it only appeared to do so; as grownups we actually *gave* our freedom away.

The marriage myth tells us that the reward for marital servitude is a special kind of devoted love that is ours alone, that essentially we *own* it, as we might hoard a casket of jewels and defend it to the death against robbers. But misers live narrow, suspicious lives, fearful and shut in behind darkened windows lest thieves discover their treasure.

The enormous response to the letter's message validated our own feelings. We decided to open the windows.

We approached our newly agreed-upon freedom cautiously, but we gradually became convinced that this was the right direction for us. At first it meant being free just to be alone, take solitary excursions, or socialize with old friends and make new ones. Opening our marriage to include outside sexual relationships did not occur until much later, and then only as a natural outgrowth of our new attitudes, and unopposed by either of us. Contrary to general belief, an open marriage is not primarily for the purpose of increased sexual activity.

A return to our former way of life would be unthinkable now. All of us, our sons included, are more honest, more self-confident, and happier than we ever thought possible. We feel more relaxed with each other because we don't hide our feelings or wishes; we ask for one hundred percent of what we want, one hundred percent of the time, not expecting to get all of it, but willing to negotiate and compromise. The greatest benefit of this practice is that it eliminates doubt as to what each person really thinks or desires. It takes the mystery out of everyday human interaction and prevents misunderstanding. Trying to read another's mind only leads to wrong conclusions.

Our second cardinal rule is: Never violate another's sovereignty. I attribute the successful working of our open relationship to two things, honesty and caring. Our feelings toward each other have deepened and been enhanced by our enlarged lives. We not only have retained our own special love, but also have more persons to love and to love us. This is a difficult fact for anyone who has not experienced an open relationship to believe or even comprehend, I know, but it is true.

Helen and I have the benefits of a three-area life: our separate lives with new friends, lovers, work, recreation, hobbies, and the trying out of dormant talents—and our life together. An unexpected bonus is the vicarious enjoyment of the other's discoveries. Her new friends often become mine, and mine hers; they are of many nationalities and races, of all ages and backgrounds, each unique and interesting. Our relationships are as varied as the people involved; most are based on intellectual kinship; a few are also sexual. With friends as guides, we have become fascinated explorers of our new home, California, a state rich in variety, and later we share our finds. The spreading out of our lives has been both astonishing and exhilarating. We can see now what only a few years ago we were blind to: that by throwing off the fear of "what people would say" (old negative fantasy) and replacing it with the positive fantasy of trusting our own minds and feelings, we would discover a breadth and depth of life we never knew existed.

Opening our marriage released a lot of creative energy. Ignoring our friends' lifted eyebrows, we tackled all sorts of new undertakings. In some we succeeded, in some we failed, in the conventional sense, but we found that experiencing the undertaking is the important thing. Refusing to give in to the fear of being an amateur or a fool, enjoying the process and the learning—that is real living. Judging a result on the spot can also be misleading, for often what seems like failure now may be seen long after as success, and vice versa. Judgements, like good wine, must age.

Probably the greatest reward of our new relationship is the experience of intimacy, the deepest possible communion between two minds. True intimacy seldom occurs in ordinary polite society, where people tiptoe around one another, fearful of intruding or of revealing themselves. Centuries of custom have shaped and polished a full set of trite, ritualistic phrases and behavior that resemble friendly communication, but that actually keep us strangers to one another. Intimacy is apt to be deeper, at least easier, when both persons have similar tastes and interests, but one of the interesting gains from our new openness was our gradual loss of prejudices we hadn't known we had, leading to friendships with people we once would have passed up and missed a wealth of new ideas and experiences.

Nurturing is one of the key words for making an open relationship work. Someone who is nurtured and sure of love won't be afraid if a mate finds additional interests or loves. Getting rid of fear is the first step toward truly enjoying a love relationship. When fear is gone, fear of not being attractive enough, or of losing one's mate, then equality and freedom enter the relationship. Feeling genuinely equal to each other is one of the most exhilarating and self-actualizing situations imaginable.

The rewards of our ten years of an opened-out marriage have been immensely greater than either of us could anticipate. We have learned as never before in our twenty-two years together to live in and enjoy the present, the *here and now;* and although we know that these years are a continuation and enrichment of our good, original marriage, with its memories of shared experiences of all kinds, and its privilege of watching four lives develop from infancy to adolescence, today is the only day we really possess. Each day is a new space of opportunity and surprises, and just as there were no rules for jumping into the New when we first jumped, there are no rules now—for no one has ever been there before!

8

PLEASE WANT ME

If you have begun to put yourself in the driver's seat, perhaps you are beginning to see the pattern of your fear reactions. You may now be able to postpone your reaction long enough to use the who? what? when? where? how? why? procedure. Once this method becomes second nature, you will find a shortcut to dealing with fear just as effective. The next time timidity, or a greater fear, prevents you from being at your best, ask yourself:

1. *What am I really afraid of?*
2. *What is the worst thing that can happen?*

Almost invariably, the answers will be different from what you originally fantasized! Here is a little scenario in which nearly everyone has acted a role at one time or another. You arrive alone at a large social gathering where people are chattering in groups or in couples, but nobody pays you any attention. An awkward feeling of not being wanted comes over you. You sense, even though you know it's your imagination, that everyone knows you are there, but is deliberately ignoring you.

Then you spot a strikingly attractive woman in a cluster across the room. She doesn't notice you, either, but how you wish she would! She is the vivacious center of attention, but her circle has no break into which you might insinuate yourself. You tell yourself that you are such a dullard you'd be out of place among such brilliant company, anyway.

If this scene is uncomfortably familiar, what did you do at that point? Did you finally get up your courage, only to find the group dissolving and the lady moving toward another newcomer, so that your intruding would be awkward and rude? Timing is often all-important in human interaction; magic moments have a short life. And time is generally lost because of fear to speak or act promptly and spontaneously.

But suppose when you first entered the room and began to imagine that everyone was deliberately shunning you (a negative fantasy), you had quickly asked yourself: *What am I really afraid of?* The true answer would not have been vague and confused like your feeling, but just one thing: *rejection.* Except for the fear of death, probably this is our greatest fear. We are all intensely afraid that others will not like us, but if they do, we then fear they will eventually abandon us—a double bind!

We turn to others for assurance that we are worthy. If others' attitudes show we are OK, then we can relax and believe in ourselves temporarily. Yet even though we crave that affirmation above all else, often we are afraid to risk finding it out; the answer might be negative. Therein lies the danger. At this crucial point you must decide whether to take a chance on learning an unwelcome truth, or to play it safe and stay ignorant. The stakes are your future well-being.

Giving in to your fear of rejection is destructive because it can prevent you from acquiring a new friend, a new lover, a new spouse, or a new job—and all kinds of other new experiences. It can inhibit your natural warmth and spontaneity, so that you appear cold and unfriendly. Thus a vicious circle is created out of sheer fantasy, out of a fear that has no basis in fact, and the very person you wish to attract is repelled by your aloofness.

Stop for a moment to analyze rejection. Does rejection lie in the other person's behavior, or in your head? If people refuse to accept your friendship, who is the loser, they or you? You know what a nice person you are; they will never know. You might better ask that person, "What is *your* problem, that you want to reject me?"

Only you can reject yourself. Only by accepting as true some other person's hastily formed and inaccurate impression of you can you be rejected! Feeling rejected is just another way of confirming your negative fantasies of your own unworthiness. It is the "I'm going out in the garden and eat worms" syndrome. It is the martyr impulse, without the cause worth suffering or dying for. It is the resentment and hatred of those Big People of your childhood who told you you were no good.

So while you are wasting energy on these negative fantasies, the attractive person at the party eludes you. Yet the chances are a hundred to one that she or he would have greeted you kindly. Why? Because an individual is not admired and sought after for being haughty and disdainful. Such a person is quick to sense shyness in a new acquaintance, and undoubtedly has the empathy, imagination, and skill to know how to put the stranger at ease. He or she is certainly not to be feared.

The second question: *What is the worst thing that can happen?* begins to answer itself. It obviously isn't death or injury, ridiculous as that may sound, except that we often behave as if it were. No, the worst thing, probably, is that she will smile, say a few polite words and walk away, an outcome that you can turn into a personal disaster, or merely a brief try that didn't get off the ground. Do you see how, in the final analysis, all your encounters, brief or lasting, with other human beings are interpreted and judged in your own head? Their importance is as great or slight as you yourself decide to label them. Whatever discomfort you feel after taking a risk in a new situation will arise not from externals, but from within. Put that marvelous instrument, your brain, to better use than creating negative fantasies!

Meeting the Unmet

For weeks, Connie felt a coolness in her husband, George. It started when he began working overtime and coming home too tired to talk, or take her out, or even have sex. She was too timid to question him (for Connie's self-esteem is fragile, always taking its cue from other people's moods) and she grew silent, too. All her feelings of inadequacy rushed back, and now she suspects that George is spending time with another woman. As he walks through the door tonight, late as usual, her suppressed jealousy boils over, and she flings her accusations in his face.

George has two choices. He knows the charge is untrue; he has been working, not having an affair. He can become angry and defensive (this would be a typical response), and the result is a family row, with stored-up resentments hurled back and forth. Or he can refuse to relinquish his inner power, and ask himself if there is a grain of truth in what she says. Maybe he has been staying away more than the job required because he finds his wife a little hard to take these days. He hasn't been with a woman, but he's thought about it! Technically, George is innocent, but he feels guilty nevertheless. Explaining himself would be difficult and painful, especially while Connie is in her present agitated state.

Their problem is that each has *unmet needs*. The needs to feel loved, wanted, and worthwhile, if unmet, are the real causes of discontented, unhappy lives. Throughout history, people fortunate enough to have those needs fulfilled have found it possible to get along happily with only a minimum of their material needs met, but unfortunately the reverse is not true.

Honest communication is Connie's and George's only hope of working through their difficulties. They each have unmet needs which they must identify and reveal. She wants companionship and reassurance of his love, he wants appreciation for working long hours, and they must *tell* each other what they want, instead of being hurt that each can't read the other's mind. (Ask for one hundred percent of what you want, one hundred percent of the time!)

Honest communication is always painful and scary, at first; but once opened up the going gets easier, and it usually results in a cleansing sense of relief and closer understanding. Even if the couple finds themselves completely at loggerheads, they will at least better understand their own and the other's feelings. Professional help is advisable then, to bring out the deeper reasons for their conflict. Should even this fail to resolve their problems, separation or divorce may be preferable to continuing in a state of frustration and unhappiness

Pressure

A fashionable affliction today is to be "under pressure." Along with the stylish ulcer, it is considered synonymous with having achieved an elevated degree of socioeconomic success. Pressure, however, is simply fear, and like all fears is nothing but a negative fantasy. It is just one more instance of what happens when you allow your self-esteem to falter and give away your inner power to another person or situation.

Your boss assigns you a job to be completed by a certain time. You have performed similar work once before, but now your body tightens. One part of your mind says "Relax, you can do it!" but another part says "This time he'll find out how incapable I really am." As the deadline nears you grow more tense, making mistakes that cause delay, until you are frantic. Then suddenly, to your astonishment, the job is done. You and your fellow workers would have been spared all that anxiety if you had believed in yourself in the first place.

A factor in the problem of pressure is the deadline (even the word has an ominous ring). To overcome the tension caused by pressure (fear), map out the work plan. Break down the task into its separate parts, arrange them in logical order, and then commence. Banish all those negative fantasies by creating positive ones of finishing the task on schedule and with distinction.

Pressure is always internal. Even if someone is pressing you to accomplish something, that feeling of being under pressure originates in your internal response—in how you *choose to react.* You can choose to keep your own cool head. Ask yourself if it is possible to get the job done. If the answer is a well-considered, objective *no,* then negotiate for better terms or an end to the proposal. If the answer is *yes,* ask yourself if help is needed, and firmly explain your reasons and ask for help if necessary.

Be aware that the person pressing you is probably also under pressure and is passing along his or her anxiety to you. When you realize how vulnerable are those who intimidate you, you can see yourself in a different light. You may be at the bottom of the pecking order, but it's no different at the top!

Self-esteem is the magic ingredient that dissolves all our fears of rejection and failure, and yet most of us have had our self-esteem severely damaged by the emotionally contaminated upbringing that is traditional in our society. As adults, we can restore our own self-esteem; in fact, we are the only ones who can do it. Recognizing that our fears are nothing more than negative fantasies, we can choose to replace them with gloriously positive fantasies of loving acceptance and success.

For someone who has low self-esteem, this may seem an almost impossible assignment. However, the truth is that the positive fantasies (which may seem like make-believe at first) take over and create the very self-esteem we sorely need. It is just a matter of practice.

In the course of improving our own fantasies, we find to our amazement that those about us are looking and acting much more cheerful and contented. It is easy for someone who feels good about herself or himself to communicate that sort of feeling to others. The happy result is that soon one's whole environment is improved. There is really no limit to the power of positive fantasies.

9

ALAS, IN WONDERLAND

The complex economy that enmeshes us today was formed from the collective fantasies of America from colonial days to the present. Its original impetus was the need to provide the fundamentals of food, shelter, clothing, transportation, and the like. As one inventive fantasy spawned another, the system expanded in an unforeseen way. No longer was filling basic needs the all-important goal. As soon as most families could take these for granted, they were induced to yearn for luxuries, and one generation's luxuries became the necessities of the next. Granted that they might have intrinsic value and usefulness, the luxuries also fed a psychological need in each purchaser: to raise his or her self-esteem and, in this one respect at least, to feel as good as the next fellow.

Americans today live in a technological wonderland, where each new invention is designed to remove them a little farther from the reality of the earth and its forces. All improvements on preceding designs are aimed at removing the human hand and mind from contact with the mechanical object's vital parts and operation. The "human element" is suspect, and less to be trusted than a well-running machine. Year by year, each device becomes more complicated and more automatic, while its human operator understands its workings less and less. Indeed, few people *want* to know. Perhaps the ultimate goal is 100 percent automation, mindless and decisionless, merely to press one master button and immediately all living creatures and all machines around the world would go into their programed jiggling and dancing, like a giant mechanical toy.

Possibly this is an absurd projection, but it may be no more so than the distance we have already removed ourselves from the reality of our source, the earth, and our own innate feelings. Without a doubt the most powerful influence on our minds, emotions, and behavior is our present society and its economy.

Competition has replaced cooperation in the Western world today. Power has made the goals of the marketplace the new morality. "It's good business" is the irrefutable last word, the incontestable argument for supporting a bad project or opposing a good one. The arithmetic of profit and loss is all that matters, and to hell with justice, human needs or suffering.

Your job, with almost no exceptions, is ruled by the law of competition. Whatever your company turns out, whether goods or services, is geared to the principle of making it better than any other company, or *apparently* making it better. You are likewise straining to do better work than your fellow employees, and they than you, or *apparently* better. Conning and bluffing are intrinsically part of the system.

You, the worker on the job—at a desk, in a truck, in a foundry—are continually under pressure from above. You struggle along, filled with the fear of failure. You may believe your discontent is your own fault, that you are lacking in character or ability, or that you are somehow less qualified than others to fit happily into the system. These suppositions may be true, but chances are that they are not. Most people feel exactly as you do! Most of them are either bored or anxious or both, but after enough time these feelings go underground, and people come to accept a continuous state of discontent as the norm.

The time is ripe for each of us to take a good look at where we are and where our country is today. While millions are still unemployed, struggling merely to exist, millions of others are spending precious lifetimes at work they despise. And for what? Why, the superfluous trinkets and baubles that the corporate economy has trained them to believe they must possess!

Families who slave to acquire a camper, a boat, and a summer cottage usually find that the husband has to moonlight in addition to his regular job; the wife must also work, and the result is that they have little time or energy to enjoy anything. Their chief satisfaction lies in *ownership*, not use, and in keeping up with their friends, who are probably also working too hard for something they do not need or cannot enjoy.

We Americans are caught up in possibly the greatest irony of all time. Owning the richest land in the world, and living under the most (theoretically) idealistic government system, after two hundred years of believing paradise was forever, we are suddenly staring reality in the face. Yesterday's larder has stopped overflowing, the bottom of the barrel shows, and all those never-ending natural resources aren't natural any more. Shortages, drugs, delinquency, crime, inflation, divorce—these are the new reality.

But most alarming of all, we are not responding to these disasters in a clear-eyed, positive, and compassionate way! We seem collectively to have given up, and we hide behind cynicism and fear. The self-righteous middle class barricades itself in suburbia, but draws its wealth from decaying cities, which are prisons for the poor. Protests from every minority are frequent, but they produce only lip service and promises. Have we ever been so divided, so fearful and hateful of each other, so lacking in cooperation?

The terrible reality is that nothing has changed, even though not to change means total disaster to all of us, and sooner than we think. Each of us individually and all of us collectively have the answer to our enormous problem.

This country cannot survive such divisiveness. The impetus for change must originate in the mind of each concerned individual. We cannot wait passively for an "expert" to come up with the foolproof plan that will start the process of change. Though all change begins with one fantasy in someone's mind and grows from that first seed-thought (the awesome power of fantasy again!), other minds must be receptive and must also have been working toward that change.

I invite you to join me in my positive fantasy. It is idealistic, and I want you to be fully aware that it is idealistic! Idealism is the most beautiful, marvelous way of fantasizing that is possible to the human mind. We perceive that something is wrong and unjust; then, by letting our minds run free in a positive fantasy, we can find the remedy. That is all idealism is: to see clearly the best solution to every problem, the finest dream for all people. Should we settle for less?

My positive fantasy of a society that cares for all its individual children, women, and men is that it be *organic*. I see it growing from sturdy roots at the bottom, like an oak, sending its life juices upward throughout all its branches, twigs, and leaves, no part more important than another and each dependent on all.

Our present society is not organic; it is contrived. It doesn't respond to needs in a natural, organic way. It *creates* a need, then supplies it at a profit. An organic society would, first of all, *care*. Caring for each other ought to be one of the fundamental purposes of any group of people. An ideal society would care about everyone: people of all skin colors, people who are poor, people with physical and mental impairments, people born more than fifty years ago, the people born female. It would also care about those who are born *male*. In essence, it would grant everyone a share of respect and dignity.

The mechanics of change may seem overwhelming at first, but that is a negative fantasy I do not accept! Once the *desire* to change is strongly felt by enough individuals, the *method* will be no problem. Once a decision and a commitment are made, seemingly impossible tasks almost always prove less difficult than they first appeared.

All that is really needed for change is for all people to feel good about themselves! External trappings are not needed when our internal self-belief is confident and strong. Then a passion to houseclean our disordered social and economic system, to get rid of the mess we have created, will infuse the country with more than enough energy to finish the job. Motivation—that positive fantasy— always provides energy! And with millions of minds creatively fantasizing and cooperating, it is absurd to fear that anything is beyond our capabilities.

Your fantasies will be different, I know, but here are some of mine.

Work will be cooperatively shared (including the so-called menial jobs), with no one unemployed who is able to work. Work that challenges a worker's ability and gives satisfaction will replace the present fragmented, dehumanizing factory assembly line. Production will be limited to what we actually need, thus preventing the unnecessary depletion of raw material and energy. Working hours will shorten accordingly, and leisure hours increase. Educational, cultural, travel, and recreational opportunities will be available to all the people, not just the relatively few. Children will get to know their fathers, and fathers their children, for a new concept of male/female relationships will arise as family life becomes cooperative. Many families and older or single persons will join together in collectives, sharing domestic work, child care, and companionship, much like primitive tribal villages or the large family units of our past. Women will then be free, as men are today, to have both fulfilling careers and well-nurtured children under this sensible and caring arrangement.

It is absolutely imperative that we put a worldwide brake on our mad, suicidal rush to destruction. I don't need to repeat the knowledgable warnings about ecological devastation, nuclear holocaust, exploding global population, and world hunger. All are sheer horror, but *they need not be inevitable.* Every one of these disasters originates, directly or indirectly, out of *private, personal fear of not being worthy.*

I see humanity's future journey as a progression of stages resembling those of the rockets which launched our spaceships to the moon. We're now in the first stage, hurtling to our destiny, every last one of us aware that we are traveling in a social vehicle that *must change* before it destroys us. If we can break free of our fears, they will drop away like the first stage of the rocket, and we will advance to the second stage, the period of creative cooperation.

Creative cooperation requires honest and open communication, devoid of fear. In this second stage of our human journey, I see workers and bosses sitting down together and discussing plans and problems in an atmosphere of equality and goodwill. The essential ingredient for achieving this successful communication is *protection.* Each participant must by general consent be able to speak freely and still be protected from censure, ridicule, physical abuse, demotion, or discharge. Without this protection for all members, bosses included (they are not immune to fear), any so-called group meeting is a sham. It wastes time and does more harm than good.

A radically different approach to productive communication is the collective meeting. Unlike most office meetings, it is not conducted by a boss, unless one is democratically selected. Instead, a different leader is chosen each time by majority vote or some other impartial method. Ground rules are established which carry over to all meetings: total equality for all regardless of rank, and freedom of speech with protection for all.

The first order of business is the leader's invitation for members to voice any stored-up resentment, misunderstanding, or suspicion they may hold toward any other member of the group. By the rules of the collective meeting, the person for whom the grievance is felt is not to respond at that time, but to listen quietly, then digest the facts at leisure. Since the complaint or suspicion is given in a calm atmosphere, under the eyes of the whole group, it is usually well thought out, not hostile, and possibly justified. The recipient may be surprised and unaware of the other's feeling, and often learns something new about himself or herself. Or the complainant may have been mistaken. In either case, rational, adult communication clears the air.

The group's purpose in asking that all resentments be aired is a healthy one. Trust and cohesion are impossible if some of its members harbor smoldering resentments toward other members. Equally important, because one of its goals is the personal growth of each member, is the fact that keeping fears and resentments hidden inside one impedes that growth.

The underlying principle which makes the collective meeting work is the purposeful elimination of fear. People do not express themselves honestly when they are afraid, but they can never achieve a confident, give-and-take intimacy and equality with others if they conceal their true feelings and thoughts. As long as the typical bargaining session between management and labor today is characterized on both sides by suspicion and manipulation, honest cooperation toward mutual goals will obviously be impossible. But cooperation and the elimination of fear between factions within groups, just as between private individuals, are essential to achieving the ideal society.

The third stage of our journey—with fear gone and cooperation a universal reality—will be the time of creative thinking and planning. What unexpected, undreamed-of innovations the fantasies of many minds will hit upon in that distant third stage are beyond anyone's power to foresee.

We have never been able to test this fantasy, for we have never had a human population uncontaminated by fear. Our cleverness has mainly been devoted to combating fear. We have made life needlessly complex. For in all the maze of living, only two simple restrictions are needed. They cover all possible conditions, events, or plans. The first one I have mentioned before: *Never violate the sovereignty of another human being.* The second is: *Do not say, do, or make anything that is harmful to children.* I mean actual children, of course, but I would also extend this nurturing protection to include the child that lives in all of us.

10

PEELING THE ONION

Our two greatest fear-mongers are government and religion.

Fear, though well-camouflaged, is rampant in government. While heads of governments and surrounding lesser figures struggle to hold or acquire more power, all are driven by an underlying fear of failure to achieve their personal ambitions. Many do not recognize this force as fear, or that it derives from secret, submerged personal doubts of their own worth. Only by climbing higher than ordinary men can their holders assuage these ravaging doubts. Is it not appalling to consider that the lines of power and the destiny of humankind, its fate of peace or war, are manipulated ultimately by the private fears of private individuals?

Meanwhile the web of fear fans out, to defense plants building every conceivable weapon, to furtive agencies employing spies and assassins, and to secret laboratories where the country's most creative scientific brains concoct methods of death too ghastly to be revealed to the people whose taxes pay for them.

Magic words are used to reassure taxpayers who might otherwise object to such undignified and even sub-human behavior. These emotionally loaded words are as valuable as warships, planes, or divisions of infantry. The language of governmentese is brilliant in its ability to euphemize murder, war, and violence by substituting *defense, preparedness, unilateral parity, nuclear strike capability, overkill, defoliation,* and so on, ad nauseam, until they sound respectable.

But all are tainted with the poison of fear, all imply that doom is impending (think what the word "defense" literally means), and all are filled with suspicion of and hatred for another country, both being products of fear. Thus in one of many ways is a nation's people taught to distrust its own intuitive, basic belief in the good intentions of common people of other lands, and to relinquish its capability of insisting on world peace to supposedly wiser higher authority.

The structure of our government resembles an onion. Sacrosanct layers surround sacrosanct layers, but when we look at government and peel away all the layers of bureaus, agencies, and departments, with all their rules, regulations, edicts, and quasi-legal pronouncements, and all the layers of legislative bodies arguing at cross-purposes, and the layers of intricate court structure whose sole function is to untangle the mistakes of that enormous band of bureaucrats and legislators and the mistakes and crimes committed by desperate, frightened citizens— when we have peeled away the last layer, we find *nothing.* We have created this impossible, hollow monster to be a parent! All the sanctity we have bestowed upon government arises out of the universal belief that ordinary people must have a leader (parent) because they are essentially children lacking the wisdom to manage their own affairs.

In a world of 100 percent potent citizens, government and leaders would be unnecessary. Do you honestly believe that because a man manages to be elected to the White House he thereby knows better than you how your life should be lived?

There is no reason to believe that what is must continue to be. Our government was created out of the fantasies of the Founding Fathers and developed from the fantasies of their successors. It can be changed by our fantasies!

We are told that government's primary function is to protect us from danger, like war and crime. Yet since the Spanish-American War of 1898 we have fought in five wars, with an average of less than sixteen years between them. Nor has the government a solution to crime, which rises steadily. Officials (federal, state, county, city) deal with crime *after* the fact; the causes of crime are too complex and the solutions politically too controversial to be attacked other than by campaign oratory.

A world of truly potent individuals would have no need of the Great Parent, for each individual's potency would sustain and nurture its owner, and therefore none would be a threat to any other. Government would then become self-government, a joyous, fulfilling way of life, oppressing no one. (Granted that such a condition is utopian, not in the sense that it is impossible, but in the sense that it is beautiful! Without the vision of what we *could* reach, how can we ever arrive, or even know the journey was worth the taking?)

Until then, what do we have? Do we have the reality of Lincoln's own utopian dream of government of the people, by the people, for the people? It would be ludicrous to say we do. We have instead nine-digital numbers for virtually every man, woman, and child. Originally intended to facilitate Social Security record keeping, they now identify potential military personnel, workers' time cards, private bank accounts and insurance policies, and who knows what else, now or to come?

Reporters are jailed for refusing to disclose confidential sources of information in their investigative work. Without the protection of confidentiality, future sources will fear revealing facts crucial to the public's welfare. Yet certain officials, for whatever obscure or sinister reasons, use their power to thwart this revelation of the truth. Those reporters who choose prison over betraying their informers are showing true potency, for they are standing firm on the principles they believe in.

A grudge-bearer can anonymously inform the Federal Bureau of Investigation of a crime, or the suspicion of a crime committed by you, *without your knowledge.* Action against you may or may not follow, but unless you go to great lengths to expunge this information, it will lurk indefinitely in FBI records. Years later, these lies may pop out to disqualify you for credit, security clearance, or whatever you may be requesting. Official wiretapping of telephone conversations, secret electronic devices for eavesdropping in private rooms, police entry under "no-knock" laws which further violate a citizen's right—are more examples of government oppression needed?

I am not disparaging the United States of America, a charge made frequently by persons who do not understand what I am saying. I love this country, and for that very reason it hurts me to see its original nobility degraded. It is the actions of its degraders that I so strongly object to, the words and actions that are eroding our freedoms and our potency. They are the fearful ones. Protectors of the kingdom, I call them, the scared little people who build up layers of restraints that will prevent a new idea from penetrating the sanctity of the established order. It is fear that causes oppression, in government as in any other place.

11

HOTLINE TO GOD

From the beginning of time, human beings have been curious about everything. When the human mind does not understand something, it creates a set of fantasies to explain it. Looking with wonder at the world around them, the early humans devised a set of fantasies that we call religion to explain what they did not understand. These fantasies were designed to show our place in the universe and to spell out the behavior that will assure our safety and protection, as well as to describe the dire consequences of failing to behave in the prescribed ways. Thus did religion become a peddler of fear with even more pervasive influence than government on the lives of most of us.

Modern-day religion is as much an intricate structure of fantasy as the mythology of our primitive forebears. But like all fantasies, it can be either constructive or destructive. Religion's positive fantasies underscore all that is beautiful and uplifting to the human spirit: the desire to be loving and kind, to be forgiving and understanding, to help the sick and the unhappy, to be honest and law-abiding, to improve oneself and develop one's talents, and to seek inspiration and deeper understanding of the origin and destiny of humankind.

But when religion (organized religion, generally speaking) moved from positive to negative fantasizing, from being a comfort and an inspiration to being a foreboding institution of fear and inflexible regulations, then it became an oppressive monster.

The early days of a new idea taken to heart by a small group of enthusiasts are filled with spontaneity and sincerity. Much love and cooperation flow mutually through the group. (A new concept is very much like a newborn child: it is born one hundred percent potent and uncontaminated by doubts and fears.) But soon the group grows, rules are formulated, and the original tenet of equality for all is forgotten as the ambitious move into power positions. The structure of an *institution* begins to form. Expansion and elaboration of the structure proceeds rapidly. A hierarchy becomes apparent, and the new rules are soon being dutifully supported by quiet masses who have virtually no power at all.

Having given up their power, the people submit to all edicts imposed from above. The rules spring from an authority seemingly far wiser than they; some pronouncements seem to issue from the mouth of God Himself (where, indeed, it's often stated they originate!) How could they doubt these superior beings with their chummy, instant hotline to God?

This elaborate ceremony might be dismissed as mere theatrical entertainment, a harmless diversion from the humdrum week, if it ended there, but it does not. The combination of majestic sights and sounds is the psychological backdrop that holds the powerless in bondage to strict obedience out of guilt and fear. The powerless do not know this, for if an outsider should question the purity of the church's reasons for pomp and ceremony, the answer would probably be that the weekly celebration imbues a feeling of peace and contentment and communication with God, and nothing else.

But that "else" in reality exists, and therein lies the enormity of the effect of organized religion, for the foundation of all but a very few organized religions rests on the fantasy that all human beings are sinners. No idea could be more false or more destructive of the human spirit.

The psychology behind this belief is extraordinarily effective. One cannot help being impressed, however sadly, with its shrewdness and simplicity. Tell a man or woman—better yet, tell them when they are impressionable children—tell and convince them that they are born full of Original Sin and that the only way to escape the hellfires of eternal damnation is to obey to the letter every edict of the church. What a superb piece of strategy! Once you have convinced them, and that is easy if you start with a child, everything else falls into place. Fear will drive them to donate generously to the church; to refrain from attending other denominations' churches (lest they hear contradictory ideas); to believe that sexual impulses are essentially sinful except for procreation; to avoid thereafter the use of birth control measures; and to believe that marriage and reproduction are their duty, but that once married, no matter how miserably, they are never to divorce and remarry—(to name a few of the many restrictions upon the human spirits of the faithful).

This assault upon human beings' rights to determine their own lives is backed up by long tradition, but it is still unfair and destructive. Through fear, it instills a distrust of individual intelligence and feelings, and promotes a dependency on outside rules and custom that are not to be questioned, a condition that can only destroy much of the total potency which is every individual's birthright.

Sympathizing with victims *keeps them victims!* Stop!

Like all victims, religious victims exist in a state of powerlessness. They *agree* to their victimization by accepting the role of sinner, and submitting to their supposed superiors. Thus they give their power away. Many a church survives through unending reminders that all humans are sinners. Because of that implanted guilt, few dare to protest. Fear holds them in the familiar rut of non-thinking and nonacting.

Religion based on fear is oppressive, but a spiritual belief born out of positive fantasy provides space for the emotional, mental, and spiritual growth of its followers by encouraging them to create beautiful fantasies that suit their particular needs and capabilities. Such a religion does not counsel people to toss their responsibilities and problems at God, but to use their own problem-solving brains. Such a religion does not impose dogma, nor use fear as a weapon to influence its followers. Even this positive fantasy of religion has one characteristic in common with the others: It is parental in its function. The question is, do we need another parent?

Many do, I know, and I would not demean their fantasy of God or their need for that fantasy. Millions of people need and rely upon it, and I respect both their need and devotion. Many others have come to temper their total acceptance of traditional religion with thoughtful inquiry. They have questioned, and rejected, dependence upon leaders and regulations that use fear and oppression to maintain a hold upon the laity. They have transferred their response to religion from the Child part of their minds to the Adult. It is a matter of the personal choice of each one of us as to which is the more comfortable.

12

OPPRESS ME NOT

Oppression has two forms. External oppression derives from an outside force too powerful to be resisted, such as an aggressive country with superior weaponry—or an angry parent. Internal oppression results from a choice on the part of the oppressed.

Jane wants to go shopping and leave her small son with her neighbor for the day. Ellen, who has no children, has planned to wallpaper the living room, then take a leisurely bath before getting dinner, neither of which is possible with boisterous Tommy around! But Ellen is a "nice" woman. She feels guilty at having more freedom than Jane and, suppressing her true feelings, agrees. Then she spends the day alternating between resenting Jane, feeling guilty at her resentment, and hating herself for bowing to another person's desires when they conflicted with her own. This is internal oppression and it is self-imposed.

If we recognize the source of internal oppression, it is easier to resist. Oppression seldom looks like itself; it masquerades as wisdom, authority, divine law, civic duty, long-suffering virtue, charm, parental pride, friendship, or even love.

When you say yes because you fear to say no, you are oppressing yourself. On how many dull committees have you served because you thought the askers "wouldn't take no for an answer?" The overly generous host who insists on pouring you one for the road, and the salesman who tries to soften you up with flattery are also giving you an opportunity to be oppressed. Are these incidents trivial? No more than drops of water that wear away a stone. These, and a thousand more, make up a steady barrage of negative incidents that can wear away your freedom and your sense of worth.

Almost all of us do our share of small-scale oppression, and in turn we let others oppress us, without being aware of what is happening. We comply with oppressive demands to avoid feeling guilty. We are all such "nice" people that we don't want to hurt anyone's feelings, ignoring the toll this behavior takes on us.

Some people in childhood make a subliminal but permanent decision to become everybody's friend, the good sport who never turns down a favor for a friend, no matter how inconvenient. These people give away their power, and they learn too late that the gift brings no genuine rewards. Those who give away their power find that the more they give, the more is expected.

Any attempt to influence someone by exploiting that person's generous feelings is dishonest and oppressive. But to go along with this attempt is to collude with the would-be oppressor and give away rightful power. When two people disagree, the only honorable course is for both to state exactly what they believe and feel and want (ask for 100 percent of what you want, 100 percent of the time!) and then arrive at a mutual conclusion. Getting things out in the open, however painfully, in the long run brings understanding and removes the possibility of oppression.

A leader-and-group situation is almost always a classic example of oppression at work. Board meetings, classrooms, PTA and church meetings are prime observation posts. A skillful leader can manipulate the gathering often without its being aware of the fact. At best, the group may feel outwitted only because it believes the leader possesses superior knowledge and authority. Then the group is colluding with the leader to bring on its own failure to gain its desired ends. It may be afraid of the chairman or the teacher; it takes nerve to speak out against established authority, and most of us would rather suffer silently than risk public embarrassment.

The collusion here is the tacit agreement by the group that *the leader is in charge*. This arrangement should be avoided whenever possible, and it can be where power is fairly equal. When it is not equal, as in sessions where an employer uses money to keep his employees fearful, the latter have only their ingenuity to gain their goals.

In a democratic, collective-type group, no one has more authority than any other. A leader exists only to guide the discussion toward a preset goal, and she or he can be challenged at any point. Any member can say, "Stop! I don't like what you just said. Please explain yourself." The resulting airing of differences is a healthy and enlightening experience for both dissident and opponent.

Children are without doubt the most oppressed single group of human beings on earth. We oppress our children when we say "Eat your carrots, they're good for you!" forgetting how we loathed certain vegetables as a child; we oppress them when we jerk a book out of their hands and order them to mow the lawn, forgetting how we once lost ourselves in a story's illusion; and we certainly oppress them when we yell at them and spank them, forgetting the humiliation we felt when we were spanked. A husband or wife who received such treatment would have grounds for divorce, but unfortunately, children cannot divorce their parents.

Adolescent sons and daughters are not spared oppression. We tell them their hair and clothes are dreadful, their rooms revolting, and their manners unspeakable, (would we dare say the same to a friend?) then we wonder why our children are rude and uncommunicative. We insist they attend school even after we both know it's become a boring waste of time.

How many doctors and lawyers are in their parents' professions because of pride and family tradition? How many family companies do children enter because of family expectations? How many children are made to feel obligated to fulfill the unrealized ambitions of their mothers or fathers?

Such parents are extremely well-intentioned and sincerely believe they are doing their very best for their children. They may not be aware that their influence is severely oppressive, even though subtle and well-meant. Perhaps out of an unconscious wish to extend their own talents and achievements beyond their lifetimes, they try to plan their offspring's lives. They disregard their children's aptitudes and preferences, discount their ability to make decisions, and deny them the pleasure of challenging life on their own, including the right to make mistakes without fear of censure.

It is not easy for either a loving parent or a loving child to perceive that this oppression is unintentionally masquerading as love. Children of highly successful parents often set themselves impossible goals in striving to meet their parents' standards and expectations. Then, long after the damage is done, they become aware that they gave away their potency in a misguided effort to please.

The Oppression of Minorities

Until recently, this country's complacent majority, busy with its own affairs, spent little time thinking about minorities. Generally, minorities "stayed in their place." During the last twenty years, however, the word *minority* has acquired a new meaning. Today it calls up a mental picture of a group protesting its oppression. The quiet ones are speaking out. Not only ethnic groups, but every other oppressed segment of society is calling itself a minority—women, men, the elderly, homosexuals, farm laborers—and who knows who will be next? The old numerical distinction between majority and minority is fading, for the latter's quality of being "minor" no longer lies solely in head count, but in powerlessness.

Americans who belong to the majority like to believe in the melting-pot myth, but our minorities have no such delusions. They know that as long as they look funny, talk funny, and act funny, i.e., "different," they will be outsiders, second-class citizens, poorer educated, poorer housed. poorer paid, and general scapegoats for the condescension, guilt, or outright hostility of the favored class. Nineteenth-century Irish immigrants knew this, too, but their native tongue was English and their skin the right shade, so that their grandchildren made it into the melting pot. But Filipinos, Mexicans, Puerto Ricans, Orientals, American Indians, blacks, and many others who "look funny" remain the receivers of our top-grade domestic brand of bigotry.

The powerlessness felt by an entire group of people originates in the same kind of negative fantasy as the powerlessness felt by an individual. Just as he or she may feel inferior because of a parent's continual downgrading, a group of individuals bearing in common some characteristic that sets them apart from the majority may unconsciously regard the latter as a parent, and humbly accept its low opinion of them. The minority "buys" this false verdict and takes on a permanent burden of self-imposed ignonimy, demonstrating once again the awesome power of fantasy.

But a positive fantasy can overcome a negative one. The established majority must be jogged into awareness that it will gain, not lose, by treating minority citizens as equals, since most people seldom give up a secure position out of sheer altruism.

This jogging must come from the minority groups, but first they must convince *themselves* that they are truly equal. Not equal in hating, fighting, or conniving (as so many believe to be their only recourse), but equal in self-esteem and determination to make the very most of their potentials and their lives. They must stop believing in other people's negative fantasies, be convinced that life holds an equal promise for them and their children, and that their future is not hopeless and unfair. They must be proud of their differences and proud of what they can contribute to life in America.

The task boils down to each individual's private decision to reject the negative fantasy of believing that he or she is inferior. Granted that the country's social and economic structures are infinitely complex and a multitude of factors influence our lives, I nevertheless maintain that all action *begins* at the individual level, and that passive acceptance merely perpetuates the status quo.

Man vs. Woman/Woman vs. Man

That women have now achieved equality with men is a myth believed by most Americans today. They will vociferously point out that women can vote and hold office, that they are now employed in jobs once thought inherently male, and that they are supposed to receive the same pay. These gains do show progress, but they are surface improvements only.

Lurking below the surface is that mass of unchanged feelings inherited from centuries of tradition. The essence of that tradition is that man was and is superior and woman inferior. Men may reluctantly part with, or share, an exclusive privilege—either because they are legally re-

quired to do so, or because intellectually they acknowledge an injustice—but for most of them their real feelings
remain unchanged.

Some women, too, have resisted the idea of equality.
This is not so strange when we realize that women have
been as programed as men to believe in their subordinate
position. Learned in girlhood, that position is safe and familiar, and women know how to operate within it. It gives
them security and certain benefits they fear to lose. These
women, now as in past generations, are prime examples of
adaptation to surrounding conditions. Married to men who
are physically stronger, they have to rely on intuition and
ingenuity to gain their ends while maintaining harmony.

The traditional woman, in essence, wages guerrilla
warfare. She is skilled in using devious methods: she is a
buffer between her children's misbehavior and her
husband's wrath; she saves bad news until after her husband has eaten a good dinner; she is lavish with praise of
him, even if it is not deserved; and she even fools herself
into glorying in his greater strength and her comparative
weakness. She sincerely believes it's the wife's responsibility to keep a marriage intact, and that her duty is to cater to her husband.

My fantasy is this: if people, both men and women,
could stop being afraid of what other people think of them,
and stop responding to the adaptation of what they are
"supposed" to look like, they could then accept themselves
and others as the *unique art object* that each human being
truly is—at any time of life, whether young or old, and
whether "beautiful" or "ugly" in the approved, conventional sense.

Man is also oppressed, but in other ways. We train him
to believe that to be a worthwhile man he must be successful; indeed, Americans are as obsessed with the word
"success" as with "youth". He must succeed in acquiring
a good job, a good wife and children, a house, a car, or he

is not entitled to hold his head as high as men who have acquired them. Until then he will feel powerless, but these acquisitions are supposed to make him feel powerful. So our folklore goes.

Alas, they seldom do; instead they strap him with financial and moral responsibilities that may drain him dry of any creativity he once dreamed of exploring. He may find it onerous and often frightening to be responsible for years of supplying food, clothing, shelter, and miscellany to a dependent family, and to be looked up to as brainier, more capable, and their unfailing source of strength, when he often feels perplexed and unsure. But because we also train him not to show his feelings, he conceals his doubts under a gruff, aggressive manner which the others fear to penetrate, and his wife falls back on oblique, evasive tactics.

Like most men and women, they are trained never to be direct. Frank speech was impolite, even frightening, if it provoked an equally frank reply. What the other person—a human mind in the raw—was really thinking and feeling about one might be more than one wished to know; better the white lie and ingratiating smile that drew a safe circle around one which meant "No Trespassing". So they learned to camouflage real feelings with banter and irony, or silence, rather than risk ridicule or rejection. Yet she longs for him to say, "I love you," without being asked; it would be more genuine, she feels.

Spontaneity ... the romantic tradition, born of fairy tales and half-remembered legends from the dim past of her childhood, where all were black or white—wicked witches and ogres and good princes and princesses. There were no grays; the good remained faultlessly good; the bad unredeemably wicked and they always died in the end. No princess even had to ask; she was deluged with declarations of undying love by her prince. Undying it was, too; no good person died or stopped loving; the stories all ended as the blissful pair began to live happily ever after. The Cinderella dream lives on subliminally in the woman's mind: marriage was to be the fulfillment of all wishes, and her lover the unchangingly devoted prince.

If ordinary human beings possessed the magic powers told of in fairy tales and could read each other's minds, spontaneity would be the rule, not the exception. Then they would *know* what the other person wanted or meant, and life would be simpler and sweeter. But they cannot know for sure, and guessing cannot take the place of asking. Attempting to read another's mind and guess at what each offhand remark or facial expression really means, at the same time guarding one's own private feelings, is demeaning to the dignity and self-respect of both. It is not demeaning to ask honestly and fearlessly, nor is the answer less valuable than if it were spontaneous; it may be a surprising but refreshing experience, and it certainly clears away doubts and misunderstanding. Above all, maintaining a static relationship wherein both persons fear to be open and natural will keep them forever short of becoming the confident, potent individuals they were born to be.

In their separate ways, men and women are all victims of early programing and the socializing process. Men then victimize women, women retaliate by victimizing men, and both victimize their parents by disappointing them through delinquency or neglect. The process becomes a chain reaction and extends beyond the family social spheres, to the business world, to politics and government, and every other phase of life. As a chain reaction tends to self-perpetuate, stopping it requires drastic outside intervention, and one of the most vital forces for halting its destructive power would be the total emancipation of women. It is unconscionable that half the human race is considered, and treated so, as unequal to the other half; but until all people are equal, none has true equality, and the victimization of both women and men will go on until it destroys us all.

When women are no longer our greatest source of cheap labor, housework and child-rearing being the largest area not insured by Social Security, and are accepted into every level and kind of employment, not just low-paid, bottom jobs; when the Equal Rights Amendment is not seen even by fearful, traditional-minded women as a subversive liberal plot; when couples can be open and honest, and regard each other as human beings; with men wanting real women instead of dolls (why, if not so, do older men generally choose young women in second marriages?) and women ceasing to act like helpless dolls; with husbands dropping the mask and burden of being family boss, and becoming sensitive to and expressive of their own feelings; when it is socially approved for a woman to ask a strange man for a date—not only will the millenium be here but women, *and* men, will have achieved equality! The final, official verification of that state of grace must be the day when both Democrats and Republicans (or whoever then are top contenders) each nominate two females to run for President and Vice-President of the United States of America in the same election. Why not? Men do it all the time.

13

BRILLIANT SUNSETS

Old age is a mental attitude, not a physical condition. We have all seen people in their eighties and nineties who are bouncing with energy, enjoying every minute, their minds clear and sharp. Each new idea or experience fills them with delight. We also see many other people with far fewer birthdays (not really younger) who are pessimistic, suspicious, and rigid of mind. They have bought society's myth that no one can avoid growing old.

Why do we regard octogenarians who refuse to be old as slightly whimsical freaks? Typical old age is a surrender. It is a final succumbing to all the injustices and disappointments and humiliations of a lifetime. They've grown too heavy to bear; it's easier now to let somebody else worry about them, to let the children take care of you, or the home for the aged. Give in, give up; there's nothing worth struggling for, anyway. Gray hair and wrinkles, aches, pains, and tiredness, and most of all feeling unwanted and useless—oh, what a sad thing it is to be old.

Garbage! No one forced you to accept all those injustices and disappointments. They were real enough at the time, to be sure, but you could have cleared your mind of them, and filled it with a creative determination not to let other people dictate how you should feel.

No word or act of another person should be permitted to crush your self-esteem. If a disappointment persists longer than a temporary reaction, it takes on a life of its own. The feeling grows larger than whatever caused it and uses up your emotional energy. Disappointments are only one more form of negative fantasizing that needs to be swept out of your mind.

Life consists of this instant. This is the only reality; the past is memory, the future unknown. This priceless living moment is yours to choose to spend any way you want, in doleful self-commiseration, or in the highest enjoyment and awareness. Each moment, regardless of what interferes—traffic, weather, flat tire, IRS, boss, neighbor, children, spouse—is your own instant in time, and you can do with it as you wish. Your age makes no difference. For that mysterious thing called life is patient, impartial, and all-forgiving; it grants a continuous stream of fresh, unused moments to everyone as long as breath continues.

Even if you have many years behind you and have surrendered to the myth of old age, you can still recapture control of your life, and fully experience it once again.

It took me half a lifetime to find this out for myself. I was as bogged down in traditional conformity as anyone could possibly be. But when I finally woke up and perceived myself, other people, and indeed the whole world in a radically new light, for the first time in my life I became *aware!* My senses woke up to colors, sounds, smells, tastes, and tactile sensations I'd never noticed before. I also became aware of the revealing body language that contradicted people's conventional phrases, as mine did, too; aware of the desperate hypocrisy of public personages; but most of all honestly aware of my own misconceptions and my real inner feelings.

But awareness of feelings was only the first timid step. By itself, it was not enough. I found I had to reinforce it with repeated application to every situation and every encounter with other people. I learned it was possible and far better, both for me and the others, to express what I really felt, to say no if I didn't want to do something, or yes if I did. This stage was practice, much as one learns to play the piano by practicing. I now call this stage *experience*, and from it evolved the psychological equation that describes the entire process: Awareness + Experience = Potency. Because the ultimate result of mastering this combination of awareness and experience was a tremendous feeling of personal inner potency, of at last being in charge of myself.

Out of all this has come a quality of life I could not have dreamed of once. Now I don't waste energy mulling over past mistakes, or even past successes; they are ancient history. I don't try to shape the future, either. Even in the days when I did try, the future never turned out as expected.

Expectations are fantasies set in concrete. They presume that life is fixed and orderly, which it is not. Life is fluid and ever-changing and totally unpredictable, because each person's life is partly composed of what all the other people are feeling and saying and doing. Another part is also unpredictable: the weather, floods, hurricanes, earthquakes, fires, Mother Nature herself! What is left is one's own territory, and the trick is to expand this part as much as possible. Otherwise, the first two parts will fill up all the life-space, leaving no room for independent choice.

Planning ahead can be dangerous, however, if the plan is set in concrete. Just as multiple contingency planning is imperative in large-scale projects of business or government, so too is it vital in human relations. To plan ahead without a realistic awareness of other people's desires, and a willingness to negotiate, is to set up your own failure.

Most people *plan* to become old and powerless. The

young may consciously hope that their old age will prove an exception; nevertheless they look about and see the decrepit, enfeebled elderly and, deep within, the feeling is implanted that this is the picture of their own distant future. Too few examples of vibrant, potent, long-living men and women are visible to change that feeling! The consequence is that the great majority of people program themselves to become replicas of the preceding generation's elderly members. They set their unconscious expectations in concrete, and are then unable to break out of the traditional mold, to be flexible, to seize life as and at the moment it comes, to enjoy each instant, and to hold on to their inner potency to their very last breath.

Advancing years present differing problems for men and women. In the case of women, ageism (our latest prejudice) is closely tied to sexism. Both involve women's lesser social stature. Despite the influence of women's liberation, in many places a woman's value is still primarily sexual, both in her eyes and the eyes of the world. Except for the discerning few, most men do not regard women of advanced years as sexually desirable. "Old ladies" are not in the same league with "older men." A man's gray hair makes him look distinguished, and the lines on his face give him character. A graying woman is showing her age, and her facial lines are wrinkles, or so popular opinion goes. If a man of sixty marries a woman of twenty or thirty we may disapprove, but we are still intrigued. If a sixty-year-old woman marries a man of forty, we are shocked.

Even when two septuagenarians marry, our feelings toward each are subtly different. He is asserting his natural role by becoming the head of a household, though we may secretly wonder that he didn't choose a younger woman. But she puzzles us. What does he see in her? She must have hidden wiles, or else she has money. She may still be quite attractive and sprightly, he slowed-down and set in his ways, but she's the lucky one! So our tradition-contaminated minds run.

In the working world, however, a man may worry more than a woman at signs of advancing age. His role is that of provider, and his whole identity depends upon how well he provides for wife and family. If by middle age he is not secure in a good job, he feels pressure from both above and below. Management may notice his failing vigor, and ambitious younger men show impatience with his outmoded ways of working.

An aging woman who has held a job since her youth with only modest expectations of advancement is less likely to feel the same fears. Her identity has not usually come from her job but from outside personal relationships, although some single women's lives do consist solely of their work and they are subject to the same fears as men. A typical older woman employee tends to rely on retaining her job by superior performance, by working late without extra pay, by doing the "dirty" jobs, by being submissive, by not complaining, and by not threatening the security of persons in higher positions. She is a realist and has given up expectations.

Our culture insists, however, that every man have expectations! It is un-American for a male to lack ambition, to be noncompetitive. Should he slip momentarily, our great god Advertising will prod him back into line with alluring displays of all the products his family must acquire to stay in the swim. The poor fellow does his best, though he often wishes he didn't have the weight of the family on his back, with its never-ending mortgage and car payments and dentist and doctor bills. By now, he realizes that his former hopes were a mirage and will never be attained. He thinks he might have achieved tremendous things, but he was always afraid to step out and try.

And now we find the man retiring, aged sixty-five. Being typical, he never quite made it on the job, and now even that is gone, taking with it his most important identity. He tries to enjoy his unfamiliar leisure, but unless he knew how to relish life outside of work in former days he will not suddenly discover how to enjoy it now. Most men, having buried their feelings for a lifetime, do not know how to awaken the sheer joy of being alive they all knew as small children. So the retired man, feeling lost and useless, wondering where all the supposedly happy years went, drifts on toward old age, his chief interest in life the acquiring of new aches and infirmities and talking about them.

The barrier between parents and children that was kept under wraps in the early years of the couple's marriage is out in the open now. The father's inability to create a warm, responsive, freely expressed affection between himself and his young children has not changed with the passage of time. They are still only wary strangers uncomfortable in each other's presence, with conversation limited to superficial and safe small talk. An intimate remark would be unthinkable, and embarrassing to both. The barrier of fear separates them.

The children's feelings toward their mother (depending upon how much of her own nature was subordinated to her husband's) will usually be genuinely warm, more relaxed, yet touched perhaps by a trace of impatient pity and resentment. In earlier years, being female she could express overt love and affection for her children, and she did; but also, as a female, she had the role of protecting both husband and children, each from the other. This often put her in the unpopular position of upholding what the children considered their father's unjust harshness, and they still may have unclear feelings toward her. Her present ways of overtly doting and waiting upon her husband, interspersed with habitual nagging, only confuse them the more, They long to be free of the entire irritating situation.

This is not typical of all aging parents and their children, but it does attempt to describe some fairly common problems resulting from blind adherence to traditional concepts of male/female roles, marriage, and the rearing of children. The tragedy in hapless families of this kind is that all of them thought they were doing the right thing. Both the woman and the man were sincerely motivated by all they had absorbed from their parents and society to be a team of good provider/supportive role, raising dutiful children according to prescribed traditional doctrine. Beyond that, the man was too busy and exhausted from work to enlarge his mental and emotional horizons. The woman was not expected, or even allowed, to enlarge hers, except in women's groups, all in the usual female serving pattern.

The couple arrives then at what are ironically called their "sunset" years. Alas, those years often have all the sparkle of a gray day on which the sink drain stops up and the car battery goes dead. Although leisure and freedom from child care are now theirs to enjoy, neither person is prepared by training, experience, or example to cope with leisure. Thus they flounder, perplexed and a little lost, apprehensive of what future remains to them.

Their regimen of intense concentration on their physical conditions and amplifying of every symptom often leads to the very thing they fear—serious illness or disability. Inevitably, one of the pair must die and leave the other to fend alone. The children, conscience-stricken but with sighs and misgivings, take in the survivor—for a time. I need not describe the conflicts that arise when three unprepared generations live together under one small roof; they are well-known. But one day, when the grandparent is no longer ambulatory, off she or he is sent to that modern-day institution, the rest home.

The rest home—that paradoxical name for a warehouse where the unwanted old are stored to wait for death! Some do provide excellent care and pleasant surroundings, but they are few and extremely expensive. None are inexpensive, for that matter; and unless available through foresight and rare health insurance plans, they may drain the financial resources of both patient and family. Unhappily, that old adage "You get what you pay for," does not seem necessarily to apply to rest homes. Far too many disclosures of gross negligence, or worse, keep coming to light to allow one to be complacent or reassured as to their adequacy or good intentions in the care of our elderly loved ones.

Sociologists ascribe the proliferation of the rest home to our newly mobile society, with its younger generations too gypsy-like to care for aged parents; to the high cost of housing, which has eliminated the old, small town's three-story, multi-bedroomed family dwelling; to the automatic dishwasher, washing machine, and vacuum cleaner which perform the tedious tasks we once were delighted to let spinster Aunt Jane do, or the hired girl; even to television, which provides the baby-sitting entertainment that Grandpa's storytelling once could furnish. Now, of course, the hired girl works in a factory, Ms. Jane lives in a swinging singles condominium, and Grandpa—we sent him to the rest home.

Until a better solution for caring for the infirm old is fantasized, we must presently bear with what is at hand. But even more than improved facilities and medical care, I propose that homes for our old people (lest we forget, that's most of us one day) should first of all be fun.

Why shouldn't the inmates of a rest home experience what we on the outside can enjoy so readily? I believe that a major part of nursing care should be the providing of intimacy and pleasure: parties, music, entertainment by amateur or professional actors, dancers, magicians; birthday celebrations, surroundings with growing plants, pictures on the walls, perhaps even well-behaved pets; books, newspapers, and magazines; radio and television; beauty care, occasional change of scene, cocktails before and wine with dinner; and most important of all, sex.

And, hopefully, love. Nothing is more rejuvenating than for two people to discover that each is supremely interested in the other. It is a terrific boost to the spirits that might work miracles of healing. At the very least, it would transform the last days from those of despair and loneliness into days of shared courage and trust.

As rest homes are set up now, this utopian picture is totally unrealistic. Until the human climate is sufficiently ready, however, we must continually remind ourselves of this most positive of all fantasies—the ideal society for all people, from the infant to the centenarian.

Here are some proposals that arise out of my positive fantasies.

I propose that this rich nation's federal government, without delay, set up a permanent program for adequate financial support of all elderly persons unable to work and without sufficient means to maintain a decent life.

I propose that compulsory retirement from work at sixty-five or any other arbitrary age be immediately outlawed. Physical and mental ability and personal choice will be the only criteria for deciding when to stop working, not an impersonal blanket rule imposed by a remote, faceless system. The cutoff age of sixty-five now symbolizes for millions of Americans the end of their useful lives. It is a psychological milestone where youth supposedly ends, and old age begins. The transition is demoralizing. Choosing to retire is one thing, but it is quite another to be told you are too old to work.

The housing of the elderly poor is a national disgrace. Forced to spend their last years in castoffs ranging from rural shacks to urban slum hotel rooms, these old men and women are indeed relegated to the nation's back porch. I propose, therefore, that U.S. corporations, by law, set aside a tiny percentage of their profits to construct retirement villages throughout the country: decent, pleasant dwellings, with community centers providing optional food service, recreational and educational opportunities, job placement, medical and dental care, and skilled training in healthy attitudes toward death and old age. To prevent these villages from becoming geriatric ghettos like those now inhabited by the elderly rich, houses for rent or purchase by younger families would be interspersed among those occupied by the elderly. Thus a mix of generations would occur, reversing the current unnatural and harmful trend toward a fragmented society.

All of these, my positive fantasies, could actually make old age something to welcome instead of dread. Old age can and should be healthy and vigorous, interesting and productive, respected and honored.

Never give up on these mental pictures of what your life deserves to be. Well-being in old age must be the reward for your years of labor and cooperation. Continue to be potent; continue to take charge of yourself instead of hoping outside events and other people will take charge of you. Continue to be aware of all that is happening with you and around you, and never let up on applying that awareness. Setting in motion the principle that awareness plus experience equals potency turns life around, but there is nothing mysterious about it. Many have tested and proved its practical workability. It is an ongoing mental and emotional process, and it can re-animate inner power at any age.

14

HAPPY ENDINGS

All of us share two universal events. We were born and we will die.

> Your lifetime is a visible short line between two masses of fog that stretch out of sight in both directions, left and right. The line first appeared abruptly as a small speck which lengthened slowly. Other specks also appeared abruptly nearby, and grew. Other lines were already there; they lengthen steadily, and crisscross each other. Some of them touch your line, and its course is diverted. Some of the lines blink out, vanishing suddenly. Some of the specks blink out, too. The fog covers the spaces where they were. Your line moves on, now left, now right, toward the opposite fog, touching many of the other lines and diverting their course for a time. Soon your line, too, will blink out in the nearing fog.

Western cultures are now so shielded from the world of nature that we have come to expect technology to protect us from virtually any discomfort or hardship. Millions of products are turned out daily to soften the rough edges of our existence. Mechanical and scientific ingenuity is devoted almost exclusively to producing objects that remove us still further from the crudities and vexations our ancestors took for granted, while laboratories manufacture more and more chemicals to rid us of pain and disease.

Despite all this protective padding, however, the supreme reality cannot be outwitted. It is the inevitability of death. Yet we are so conditioned to expect miraculous solutions to every problem that many of us refuse to recognize death. The subject is too distasteful, much too unpleasant to think about; we put it out of our minds, hoping it will go away.

But of course it will not go away. The thought crouches as a fear in a corner of the mind, ready to pop out at any reminder, and as the birthdays pile up the fear comes forward more often and more insistently.

Why is death so fearful? If pressed, some will speak of their dread at the total oblivion they fear awaits the extinction of earthly life. This might seem to indicate an intense awareness and appreciation of one's unique identity and the desire to prolong it and prevent its ending. We would expect persons with high self-esteem to have this attitude. But it is more likely the opposite; persons of low self-esteem may resist the thought of death because they feel unready for it. They have not yet measured up to their potential by completing or even attempting what they once hoped to accomplish.

People who fear death are generally those who are not living lives of quality! Their days are empty; Saturday resembles Monday, and Thursday, Wednesday; they are too much alone, having little contact with a wide variety of people; their emotional needs are not met; and time is an unchanging, oppressive burden. They are ruled by negative fantasies; they fear this, they fear that, and they feel worthless, unloved, and unlovable. They are caught in a vicious circle, for their fears hold them back from taking risks in new activities or human relations that could raise their self-esteem. In moments of high awareness of their predicament, they panic at the thought of their failures and the swiftly lessening time in which to make amends. Then the ultimate fear possesses them—the fear of dying, which is the ultimate negative fantasy.

A life of quality, and by that I do not mean necessarily a life of affluence, fame, or extraordinary achievement, is a life so filled by the experiencing of each instant that it has no room for the fear of death. It is a life available to the most ordinary of us. It can be a short life or long, because its essence lies not in quantity but in quality. And time being only an illusion, the length of a life makes no difference. A full and complete life can be days, months, or years long.

A religious faith and genuine belief in a hereafter comfort and reassure millions and lessen much of the fear surrounding death. Grief and sadness at separation from loved ones are still present, but the truly devout who feel they have made honest atonement for their sins do not (or should not) experience a personal fear of departing this earth. For many sincere people, religion is ideal and a necessary part of their lives; their entire concept of God as Creator and a heaven that awaits them is a beautiful, positive fantasy. Here again, their absolute conviction is another illustration of the awesome power of fantasy, a fantasy I respect and would in no way demean.

For people without traditional religious beliefs, the philosophical question might appear far more difficult. These individuals, and I am one, must find strength and support from within themselves and from others of like mind, and must formulate an intellectual as well as an emotional concept that will stand by them in rough weather as well as in fair. They have no ready-made rules handed down through time to turn to for instruction and guidance when disaster strikes, and are not in a position to accept fate unquestioningly as the will of a Supreme Being. They must struggle through with only the reasoning of their Adult, the compassion of their Nurturing Parent, and the undampened optimism and belief in self of their Natural Child, all augmented by the supportive love of others. This may seem a difficult road to travel more or less alone, but the going sharpens the mind and toughens the will! For me it is a workable way to deal with day-to-day living, and it is also my philosophy regarding the larger issues of life and death.

I do not fear death. Death is a fact. All of us deal constantly with facts; they are the warp and woof that make up the fabric of our lives, and death is simply another, the final, fact. Instead of fearing death, I accept the fact of death. Acceptance, which is a complete, unblinking acknowledgement of a fact, removes the fear one might otherwise have toward it; one faces it on equal terms, so to speak. To accept death is not merely to tolerate or ignore it, and certainly not to fear it. It is to acknowledge it unreservedly as a fact one can never change, and then to go about the business of living.

To spend precious moments and energy in fearing the cessation of your life is to shrink by that much the very life you fear to lose. All fear is destructive and the fear of death the most destructive of all, for it is completely useless. It changes nothing except the living that did not take place during this self-indulgent negative fantasy. Dwelling on apprehensions of a painful end is also indulging in a destructive negative fantasy. It is to suffer the pain before it comes (and it may not) and to die a thousand deaths before the actual event.

Our culture does not teach us a realistic attitude toward death and dying. Our language employs polite euphemisms to disguise its reality: passed on, for died; inter, for bury; deceased, for dead; at the funeral the body, not the corpse, reposes in the casket, not coffin (which has inexplicably acquired an unpleasant connotation); and the features of the dead one are cosmetically enhanced to resemble a sleeping, living person. Yet despite our reluctance to face the reality of death, it holds a fascination that impels funeral-goers, carefully observing the utmost in hushed, proper manners, to file solemnly past the open coffin and cast quick, furtive glances at its occupant. They dare not linger, for that would betray their intense curiosity and awe; they must not break the tacit agreement of those assembled that death is not quite real, and that one, as a member of the living, must join in the pretense that the funeral is a fraternal and social duty, and pertains only to a state of being, now nonbeing, thankfully removed from their own.

We, perhaps egotistically, consider ours to be the most advanced, educated, sophisticated, scientifically knowledgeable age in history, but is has not produced any clearer perception of what happens to us (if anything) after death than the mystics of any long-vanished primitive tribe. My positive fantasy is that we must be content to leave our insatiable human curiosity and wonderment forever unsatisfied, and turn to what we at least do understand to some degree, and which we do have the power to change and use to our advantage.

I've been fortunate—by never losing my sharp awareness that life consists of this instant, and by relegating the last instant, the moment of death, to its proper place in the sequence, assigning it no more or no less significance than the instant I am experiencing now—to be able to free myself of all fear of that final moment.

It wasn't always so. I used to torture myself by reliving past mistakes or worrying about the future, until I finally saw that this habit was literally robbing me of real living, and making me dislike myself as well. Getting rid of that habit and retraining my thoughts and feelings to stay in the *here and now* took practice and discipline, lots of it, but worth every bit! The resulting changes in my life and outlook would have been unimaginable to me before. Today I can honestly say that my life could not be more satisfying. I don't *need* to add to it, even though each succeeding moment adds another interesting experience in feeling or thinking or doing. If death were to come right now, I could not complain that it was cutting short a life not yet completed. I shall probably continue to live for x-number of years more, but when the right time for death does come, I should like the privilege of meeting it in the extraordinarily imaginative caring, and sensitive way shown in the film *Soylent Green.*

Soylent Green was the brilliant actor Edward G. Robinson's last film; and, ironically, one of its themes was the kindly yet practical view of death in the 21st century. Robinson's role was that of an old man who had lived a full life, but longed to leave it because the earth lay in parched ruins, a drought-stricken wasteland. He chose then to go to the "dying place" euphemistically called "going home." This was a high amphitheater where, daily, hundreds of sick and crippled of all ages entered voluntarily to receive their society's novel but humane last social service. A painless, death-inducing drug was administered, then each was asked what special comforts would make their departure most pleasurable: what favorite colors in surroundings, what favorite music, what foods, and what scenes would they like to see again? The old man, lying on a soft couch, asked only to see his beloved land as he remembered it; whereupon, across a vast screen appeared a moving panorama of the vanished forests filled with deer and songbirds and tumbling streams. He watched enraptured, happy once more, until the drug took effect and he peacefully closed his eyes and died.

What a glorious way to die, compared to our present

procedure amid sterile, impersonal hospital surroundings, with dangling tubes attached to our bodies, and the prolonging of incurable illnesses for some "ethical" reason! Or if we choose to end our lives, the scandal and stigma of suicide inflicted upon our families. *No!* I would like to have the privilege of dying in dignity and gladness, letting all the unfinished business of life slip away, the sadness I might still feel over things I wasn't able to make others understand, and the tinge of regret over things I failed to accomplish. (We all do what seems best at a given moment; if we had known better we would've acted differently.) Then, in my last hours, I would choose to see the beautiful faces of my friends and loved ones, if not on a great cinematic screen, then as images in my mind—my final positive fantasy!

I have a positive fantasy that we human beings will live to the age of two hundred years or more once we remove the seeds of destruction planted in the fertile soil of fear! We now can make ourselves sick, and program ourselves to die. The latter subject I discussed in the preceding chapter. To illustrate the former, please perform a simple experiment; Hold your left arm aloft and wiggle your fingers. Now, what made your fingers move? Was it a brain in your hand giving an order? Of course not, you say; it was my mind deciding to go along with this rather silly suggestion. You are absolutely correct; your mind is at the controls. Now, if you will, extend this experiment, in imagination, to your liver, your pancreas, your heart, whatever. What governs them? Is it not the mind again? Your conscious mind, that metaphorical tip of the iceberg, probably cannot alter their functioning; but that uncharted submerged vastness, your unconscious mind, according to many recent findings, unquestionably can. Medical authorities are already recognizing that stomach ulcers, arthritis, and migraine headaches are affected and/or caused by emotional stress. Now cancer is beginning to be suspect also, and surmised that it may occur in persons having a certain psychological "profile": a poor self-image, a reluctance to insist on fair treatment from others, suppressed anger, etc., all originating solely in the mind! Lay people, also, frequently observe personal instances of severe stress being followed closely by physical upsets and even pain. As time goes on, more and more evidence of the emotions as the source of our physical ailments will be verified, I haven't the slightest doubt, and many researchers in holistic medicine and preventive treatment are now working in this area.

Merely extending the present typical old age is not their goal. The aim is to expand the middle years, so that besides increasing vigor and capability, near-perfect health can produce many years in which to gather experience, learning, and, hopefully, greater wisdom. The notion of a population composed of a large percentage of persons one to two hundred years old, in excellent health, looking like present-day forty- or fifty-year-olds, energetic, and possessing the knowledge, skills, and insight accumulated during an extra century or more is staggering and fascinating!

I reject any doleful negative fantasy of a world of the "aged", with sour ideas and the numerical power to inflict them on the young. Even the question of overpopulation, which is immediately raised at all such speculation, I reject also. The people of the future that I see in a beautiful mental image will be different from us. They will have learned *how to eradicate fear;* indeed, they will never allow it to begin, starting with the newborn's first day. Their energy will not be directed like so much of ours, toward suspicion, fear, ill health, and despair, but toward a total development of their potentials, both mental and emotional. When all human minds are that free, I have no misgivings about their ability to work out any problems arising from an organically new society.

There would be no reason then to fear old age and its culmination, death, for one would have experienced the complete life intended at birth. To experience less, or even to demand less, is not to receive what every individual deserves by the mere fact of being born. Even today the option is there, waiting to be claimed. Only the negative fantasy of fear prevents it.

15

PERFECTION IS AN ATTITUDE

You are human, therefore, you are perfect. When I say this, as I do repeatedly in talks before audiences or on radio, listeners become confused. All their lives they have been told that human beings are imperfect. Alexander Pope said "To err is human." It is the standard excuse and consolation for any mistake, any oversight, or any instance of poor judgement. "You're only human! We're not perfect, you know." What a myopic point of view! Do you look up at a star and say "That star's not perfect!"

We human beings are made up of the same basic element as the stars: pure energy. Rocks and soil are energy, water is energy, sunlight is energy; trees, grass, flowers, birds, fish, animals are energy. And human beings are energy, in still another form. We are as much a part of the universe as the star or the most microscopic speck of animate or inanimate substance. If it is absurd and unthinkable to regard a star shining in the mysterious, dark spaces of the night sky as imperfect, why would we deny the perfection of a human being?

Ah, you say, stars (and all those others things) don't do what we humans do. They don't make mistakes, they are predictable, they follow a certain pattern. You never know what people will do, and most of the time they seem to do it wrong!

Did you ever stop to think that those very qualities, of freedom to choose, of infinite creativity, constitute perfection in human beings?

Human behavior ranges as wide as the human imagination can reach, for it is based on fantasy. We can call it bad or good, but that is only a subjective judgement. For all we know, the final tally of the antics, follies, attempts, failures, disasters, and achievements produced by all the generations of humanity will add up to a perfect summation of our part in the evolutionary process of the universe. The human beings whose strivings make up this whole are thereby no less perfect than the galaxies or the atoms.

Earthquakes, hurricanes, tidal waves, floods, forest fires, and diseases do occur. Few are predictable to any degree of accuracy that might provide protection from their forces. But are not all these merely the workings of the universe? Are they mistakes?

Only our negative fantasizing makes them so. The natural disasters occurring around the globe, incessantly and unstoppably, are but an integral phase of the changing planet. Astronomers tell us that stars collided eons ago, and are still colliding somewhere in space. Are these mistakes? Ice Ages have chilled the earth and its creatures more than once; another is predicted in a not-too-distant time. More mistakes by Mother Nature? Of course not, unless we insist on tunnel vision.

The incalculable total energy of the universe emits forces that scientists can only minimally understand or measure. Indeed, the very existence of most must be unknown. As for knowing a reason for the operation of these forces, no one has any more than an inkling of the creation of the universe. We can only look with our limited knowledge and vision at both ourselves and the vastness that surrounds us, and try to see a relation of one for the other. By definition, the universe is all we know or have. There is no other superior model by which to judge it. As the one and only, therefore, can it be anything but perfection?

On the other hand, can a perfect whole be made up of even one imperfect part? Then is not every component of our universe, large or small, including humanity, also equally perfect?

Whether or not people's present troubles will affect the final score a billion years hence, we do nevertheless live in the here and now. We cry now; we also laugh now, and laughing feels better. I don't understand the cosmic reasons for our existence more than anyone else, but I am intensely concerned with promoting all possible ways to increase the world's output of laughter.

That's why I am convinced of the perfection of every single human being on this earth. Because, being perfect, each has the power, the *potency*, to choose the life he or she wants to live.

My unshakable belief in this perfection persists in spite of what I have seen and heard in years of professional work with troubled individuals. Women who smiled too brightly, but were betrayed by a nervously tapping foot, men who grimly tightened their jaws, then finally collapsed into sobs—they were all in the grip of negative fantasies and I could feel their suffering. Others confessed acts of incredible meanness and cruelty; thwarted suicides cried out their anguish; and convicted rapists and murderers revealed their fear.

There is no limit to the perverse ingenuity of human beings to harm themselves and others. That most imaginative instrument known, the human brain, can be as destructive as it can be constructive. The awesome power of fantasy! The brain continuously creates fantasies of one kind or another. These unhappy souls chose to create negative fantasies which led to negative acts. The more destructive the act, the more negative the fantasy that provoked it.

Still I say: Each is human and each is perfect, miserable creatures hated by their fellows though they are. I believe as strongly as I believe anything on earth that it is not the man or woman who is imperfect; it is their acts which are imperfect.

These people were taught and learned too well to fantasize negatively. But because of the intrinsic, enduring perfection within each of them, hidden or lost though it seems to be, each one of them has the capacity to change. When we are willing to see perfection in others, we will see it. When we are willing to acknowledge perfection in ourselves, we will know it. Perfection is an attitude toward life.

16

SO WHAT?

Human emotions are what this book is all about: Love, friendship, compassion, caring, mirth, joy, and our darker feelings, hate, prejudice, anger, jealousy, and fear. It is especially about fear, that emotion that makes millions of us believe we are less than we really are.

We blame painful emotions on other people, or on situations we believe to be hopeless. If only he or she behaved differently, we wouldn't be jealous or angry. If only we had more money, we wouldn't tremble before the future. If only, if only. "If" is our alibi for stalling in an emotional dead center and not using our creative minds to move into happier times. Change is frightening because it takes us into the unknown. The present, however miserable, is familiar, and besides, it gives a reason to demand sympathy from long-suffering friends.

The hidden irony to all this is that *we manufacture all our emotions entirely within our minds!* Nobody can make you mad, just as nobody can make you sad, glad, or happy. You may respond to what someone says or does by becoming angry, or hilarious. But *you choose* to become angry or hilarious. Your emotion is your own; it originates in your own mind.

Even that most enchanting of all emotions, falling in

love, is created solely in your mind. Your beloved does not cause it. You cause it.

Because feelings are in your mind doesn't mean they are unreal. *All emotions are real.* It's how you react to an emotion that counts. Your response is what makes the difference between chronic discontent (powerlessness) and being in harmony with yourself and others (inner power).

It is important not to confuse powerfulness with aggression. Powerfulness is the sense of well-being experienced when you are in command of your own feelings and actions. Aggression toward others is not proof of power. Indeed, it is the extreme opposite and betrays the aggressor's low self-esteem. An individual possessing inner power has no need to prove his or her worth by domineering others.

Emotions ordinarily considered pleasant—anticipation, excitement, mirth, joy, fondness, love, sex, among many others—and all the delights of the five physical senses generate a sense of well-being and produce a sense of powerfulness.

The negative emotions belong to the powerless group, yet they may *seem* more intense, and therefore powerful. But consider the following definitions thoughtfully.

- Anger is a sense of powerlessness.
- Fear is a negative fantasy of being powerless.
- Jealousy produces a sense of powerlessness, but is not a single emotion, being a mixture of low self-esteem, envy, fear of rejection or abandonment, and anger at others and one's inability to change a situation.
- Sadness or grief is repressed anger, which produces a sense of powerlessness.
- Remorse, regret or depression is a sense of powerlessness.
- Hate is a sense of super-powerlessness.

All of us experience a myriad of emotions, good and bad. Are we then inevitably saddled with the destructive effects of negative emotions? Of course not. It is possible, by using the analytical part of our minds to halt every destructive emotion long enough to ask ourselves, "So what?"

It is helpful to understand what physically occurs in your brain when, for example, you feel angry. The stimulus rushes through the brain cells, along the same, well-worn neuronal pathway of many previous angers, triggering a surge of adrenaline through your body that sets off your old, familiar response. Your prehistoric ancestor needed that extra burst of energizing adrenaline for the "fight or flight" that allowed him to survive. Although modern dangers tend to be less physical than his, your body still retains the mechanism for the same primitive response to stress. This adrenaline-stimulated response is to react with fighting words or actions. Now, to react to another person with hostility leads only to worse relations with that person.

Anger and fear are probably the most difficult emotions to handle. First, because they usually seize us without warning, giving us almost always no time to react rationally. Secondly, anger almost always involves us in conflict with another person, which leads to further trouble. Grief, guilt, regret are companions of solitude, and the passage of time and new events usually ease them. But anger and fear may flare up repeatedly, and the easily angered or frightened individual must learn ways to handle them or forever be at their mercy. He must learn to stop short, and ask himself "So what?"

Anger is generally assumed to be caused by an external stimulus, a person or situation. It is actually, however, the angry individual's feeling of powerlessness before this stimulus. Every instance where anger results arises from the angry person's powerlessness to control inanimate objects or animals, to succeed or to change other people's undesirable attitudes or actions.

Virtually everyone has been programed to respond irrationally to anger. If someone thwarts or criticizes you, a sudden feeling of being powerless overwhelms you, which is immediately converted into anger. Then, attempting to deny that powerless feeling, you strike back, verbally or otherwise.

You don't have to *do* something just because you experience an emotion! Feel the feeling, look at it, think about it; it is your emotion and it is real, and you have the right to your emotion. But hold off acting upon it! Instead, ask yourself, "So what? What is causing it, where does it come from?"

If someone calls you a son-of-a-bitch, programing tells you to become angry and perhaps strike out with a fist. But you don't have to comply in knee-jerk fashion. Silently say "So what?" take a deep breath, remind yourself that you're not a son-of-a-bitch, then ask what is troubling your accuser and if he or she would like to discuss it calmly. Such an unexpected response will not only throw the other off balance and possibly reduce the animosity, but it will also give you breathing space to banish your own anger and prevent its stepping up the confrontation. It is the only rational way to deal with conflict between persons, or between nations, for that matter.

Keep working at it. This unaccustomed way to handle your anger requires practice and planning. Mentally rehearse situations with people who are habitually overbearing toward you and with whom you've always in the past *chosen* to be irritated. Like actual fire drills in grade school, mental rehearsals will train your responses in a new, desirable pattern, which will eventually become automatic, no matter how severe the provocation. (New neuronal pathways in your brain will deepen and bypass the old programed routes. Don't let early failures discourage you. No skill is perfected at first attempt.

Keep remembering the trusted equation: *Awareness + Experience = Potency.* Awareness is knowing how to change, and why. Experience means putting that knowledge into practice. Resolutely followed, they add up to potency, which is the calm, tension-free, unafraid, untroubled rapport with self and others enjoyed by those who have learned how to deal with those negative emotions that formerly swamped them with a sense of powerlessness.

Potency doesn't come easily, but neither is it beyond anyone's reach, for many have achieved it. Write down your goals and your trouble spots. Refer to them frequently and keep an informal record of your progress. Your scribbled notes will pay off by increasing your awareness, which being thereby steadily renewed and expanded, will inspire you to improved practice and enhanced experience.

Fear follows nearly identical lines. Every time you feel fearful, ask yourself, "What am I afraid of? What is the worst thing that can happen to me?" When you realize that the worst thing is not the end of the world, you may decide that taking a risk will open up new, exciting opportunities that far outweigh any doom your fears predict. Fearsome caution brings few if any rewards. This is the time to call upon those words that go right to the heart of the matter: So what? *Living is risking, and risking is living!*

Jealousy, without a doubt, is one of the most painful of human afflictions, partly because it is a combination of several emotions all attacking the individual at once, but primarily because it is so destructive of one's self-esteem.

A wife becomes jealous of her husband because she suspects him of seeing another woman. She is angry at him for deceiving her, then despondent as her self-esteem plunges to rock bottom because she is no longer supreme in her husband's eyes; she hates the woman for stealing what she considers her rightful "property;" she envies the woman who, she is convinced, must be more beautiful, sexier, younger, more charming, more talented, maybe even richer; she is fearful that her husband will abandon her; and finally she is angry at her own inability to change the distressing situation. Anger, fear, hate, low self-esteem, depression—small wonder that jealousy devastates its victims and inflicts them with a sense of powerlessness! It makes little difference whether the jealous person's suspicions are correct or not; jealousy over imagined wrongs can be just as intense as jealousy based on fact. Like all emotions, both originate in the indiviudal's mind.

If you were to discard stereotypical programing, and if you also possessed a serene confidence in your own worth as a human being, you would not be jealous because of a loved one's seeming defection. You might feel a momentary pang, but then you'd think "So what?" If you truly loved that person, you would rejoice that your lover was finding an additional source of pleasure and happiness. Furthermore, your relationship with your lover, unsullied by recriminations, would very likely be enhanced and deepened.

Sadness is anger repressed. Sadness over a lost love, or grief at actual bereavement, is subtly tied in with anger: anger at the lover's desertion, or anger at the loved one for dying and leaving you behind. This feeling is repressed as unseemly in the face of death, but it is there nevertheless. Because never has the bereaved one felt more powerless; despite every heroic effort to prevent it, death has won and taken the loved one away forever.

Let us imagine an extreme and terrible example. Your house burns to the ground and your beloved spouse and children die in its flames. You are left horribly alone, near-mad with grief, and penniless. You want to die yourself, at first, but the will to live will not be denied. In time you say in effect, "So what? I must go on with my life and make that life as worth living as I possibly can." And so you do, as untold numbers of bereft human beings have done before you since time began.

Depression is a feeling of powerlessness that feeds on itself. You spin your emotional wheels thinking the same discouraging thoughts over and over, a futile exercise that will never solve your problems.

Whenever you find yourself in this seemingly hopeless trap, *change channels*. Just as you turn off a boring television program by switching to another channel, switch your mind to another thought. Any thought will do, no matter how trivial. Say you're depressed because your lover has left you: *every time* you think of him, or her, instantly think of some other thing, even if it's no more than a crack in the ceiling, or garbage to be taken out, or the price of gasoline, or whether the mail has arrived. Unpleasant things, pleasant things—just as long as you change channels in your mind. Use your knowledge of the brain's neuronal pathways. Instead of digging the old pathway deeper and deeper, and stronger and stronger, start a new one! Change channels *instantly* every time your mind strays to a depressing thought.

This technique works. If you refuse to let your mind dwell for even one fraction of a second on what has been depressing you (which you can't change anyhow), you may be amazed at how quickly your depression will lift and disappear. Before long, you will be able to give a passing thought to your heartless lover without bursting in tears or vowing murderous revenge. Your memories will remain; only the pain will be gone. You will be able to say "So what? Life does go on, and it is worth living."

It's never too late to learn new ways. The adage "You can't teach an old dog new tricks" simply isn't true. Maybe it is with dogs, but you're human, with a reasoning brain, and no matter how old you are or how programed your reflexes have been, you *can* learn new ways.

Never be ashamed of an emotion, or think it unimportant. It is completely natural to have emotions, both pleasant and unpleasant. You wouldn't be human without them.

Even the so-called negative emotions are useful; they

may be giving you a message. Anger at a trifle may, if delved into, reveal the *real* source of your anger, something which you can work on to resolve. Jealousy may point up your basic insecurity, much more important than your spouse's wandering eye. Like physical pain, whose role is to alert you to trouble that needs attention, many emotions are also messengers that should not be ignored.

Above all, the most important thing is *what you do with it* after you feel an emotion! Remember, it's in your mind, belongs to you, and only you can choose what to do with it. You can react in the same old way you've been programed to react since you were a child. You can let fear paralyze you, anger get you in a fight, jealousy sour you, if you choose.

Or you can choose a way that may be hard at first because it means parting with old habits and teaching yourself new ones. It will not be hard for long. The first time you ask yourself "So what?" and, to your astonishment, suddenly know you are the boss of your emotion instead of its slave, will be thrilling. Notice how much warmer are other people's responses to this changed you; it may make such an impression on your mind that the new habit will be well-launched.

"So what?" Those are nervy words, prying words. First, they ask what's going on now? Then, what do you plan to do about it? These are questions with a relentless challenge. But they also imply an exciting possibility, a new way to live more serenely, fearlessly, honestly, joyously. A new way that waits only for a decision never again to be at the mercy of programed, self-destructive emotions. A challenge—that also holds a bright promise.

So, now what?

DREAM THE IMPOSSIBLE DREAM

This book itself is a fantasy, and its final chapter is not an ending but a beginning, a springboard, a launching pad to free our minds from earth-binding chains, to roam the galaxies, and never to allow negative fantasies to inhibit, destroy, demean, or pollute the mind of any living creature. This is your invitation to come fly with me, come soar with me, go to the heights with me—to heights that heretofore were frightening, and called impossible.

My gift of love to you is this: Never ignore or underestimate your ability to fantasize positively. Dream those so-called impossible dreams! Fantasize, for in each of you lie the seeds for the beautiful future. How you and I fantasize the future will inevitably be different. What is ideal for me may not be ideal for you. But I believe that some day in the future we can combine our different ideals in what I would call *individual collectivism,* a new society where one's individuality is not lost in the group, and where the well-being of the group is not subverted by the individual.

Fantasize, and when the urge comes over you to be cynical, hopeless, and negative, slay the Medusa! FANTASIES CAN SET YOU FREE!

About the Authors

Stan Dale is a transactional analyst, sexologist, educator, and radio commentator who provides his audiences with a forum for open and honest evaluation of themselves and the world around them.

A New Yorker by birth, Stan spent 19 years in Chicago, where he was host of several well-known talk shows, including WDAI's "Confrontation;" WBBM's "Nightline;" WCFL's all-night "Stan Dale Show;" and nine years at WLS, where he gained fame as moderator of the popular panel show "Pinpoint." Since arriving in the San Francisco Bay area, Stan has been a communicaster with KGO and K-101, San Francisco, and KZST, Santa Rosa. He has been with KSFO, San Francisco, since March, 1978, and was part of the team that won the "Broadcast Journalism Award for Outstanding Reporting" for its coverage of the killings of Mayor George Moscone and Supervisor Harvey Milk; for the past year he has conducted a two-hour telephone talk program dealing with relationships, Sunday evenings from 8:00–10:00 P.M.

Stan has a degree in Psychology and Sociology from Roosevelt University, Chicago, and The Illinois Institute of Applied Psychology. He is one of only ten worldwide recipients of the prized Mahatma Gandhi Peace Medallion for his selfless commitment to the cause of world peace, humanity and brotherhood. He won "The Humanitarian of the Year" award in 1972 from the Ethical Humanists.

Stan has taught human sexuality at Sonoma State University, Cotati, California and more recently became a faculty member of The Institute for Advanced Study of Human Sexuality, San Francisco. He is a frequent lecturer to a wide variety of service organizations, social clubs, churches, college, high school, and junior high school campuses.

He served with the U.S. Army in Korea, and received a commendation for meritorious service. He lives in Santa Rosa with his wife, Helen, and four sons.

Val Beauchamp has taught English to teenagers in Alaska, American GIs in Japan, and art to college students at the University of Washington, Seattle, her alma mater. She first became interested in oppressed people in the late 1950s when, with a small group of Unitarians, she helped to publish a bi-monthly periodical exposing the needs and problems of Northwest Indians in the state of Washington. After moving to California, she became aware of still other oppressed peoples—Hispanic-Americans and blacks, most of whom were undereducated, and fifteen percent unable to read or write. This concern opened succeeding doors: to the volunteer teaching program for illiterates conducted by the Adult Literacy Centers in Berkeley and Oakland, to a reporter's job on a weekly Berkeley newspaper owned and run by blacks and the Spanish-speaking, and to supervising the training of minority employees in the West Coast branches of a national mail order firm. These experiences and a lifelong interest in psychology inevitably expanded her awareness of isolated oppression to that of virtually all humankind, that in many subtle and self-destructive ways we all have allowed ourselves to be oppressed—majorities and minorities, male and female, young and old. This conviction led naturally to her collaboration with Stan Dale on *Fantasies Can Set You Free*. Ms. Beauchamp currently lives in Hoquiam, Washington.